Publisher's Disclaimer:

In the culinary realm, chefs and cookbook authors routinely pay homage to their inspirations and influences as a testament to the respect they hold for the diverse tapestry of culinary traditions.

This practice, deeply rooted in the ethos of culinary appreciation, serves multifaceted purposes. It is a profound display of respect for the rich traditions that have shaped their culinary journeys, recognizing the collective wisdom of those who paved the way for innovative and creative cooking.

Moreover, it becomes an educational avenue, offering readers insights into the myriad sources that contribute to a specific recipe or cooking style. Transparency is another key aspect, fostering trust and authenticity by openly sharing the varied inspirations behind each creation.

This acknowledgment celebrates the communal nature of cooking, acknowledging the interconnectedness and collaboration within the culinary community. While not always a legal requirement, it acts as a proactive measure to mitigate any potential ethical or legal concerns, affirming that chefs and authors are not claiming sole ownership over widely recognized recipes.

In essence, acknowledging culinary influences is a cultural and ethical practice that enhances the authenticity and richness of the culinary landscape, fostering a sense of community, respect, and continuous learning.

With this in mind, this book may include references to trademarks, brand names, or specific products for illustrative purposes only. Such references aim to celebrate the original and acknowledge their role in U.S. culinary history. The publisher and author explicitly disclaim any intention to use the trademarks, names, reputations, products, or intellectual property of the individuals, businesses, and/or products mentioned. The inclusion of these references is solely for the purpose of discussing the evolution of food in the U.S. from colonial times to the present. This usage does not imply any endorsement, sponsorship, or intent to infringe upon the rights of the respective trademark owners. This book is an independent work and not affiliated with the original creators mentioned, or their brands. The Author and Publisher have no knowledge of trade secrets or recipes outside of the realm of public domain.

Any similarity or accidental sameness to another published recipe is purely unintentional. The recipes presented in this collection are crafted to the best of our ability, drawing on personal experiences, culinary knowledge, and the inspiration derived from various sources. We strive to offer a unique and creative perspective on traditional and contemporary dishes. In the event that a resemblance is noticed, it is purely coincidental, and no intention exists to replicate or imitate existing recipes. Our aim is to provide readers with an authentic and enjoyable culinary experience while respecting the diversity and creativity inherent in the world of cooking. If any unintentional similarities are identified, they are not a result of deliberate imitation but rather a testament to the shared elements found in the vast and evolving landscape of culinary creation. All rights of the original owners are acknowledged and respected.

Bryd Press. Toronto. Canada. 2024

The notion of 'instant' in culinary creation is but a mirage. What we now deem as swift or timeless recipes are the refined distillation of myriad experiments across generations. In the United States, classic recipes bear witness to the fusion of diverse culinary traditions, each dish echoing the imprints of countless hands that toiled and experimented, yielding both triumphs and setbacks. Hence, relishing the flavors of a classic recipe is savoring the culmination of a journey shaped by time, persistence, and the collective wisdom of myriad kitchens.

The recipes within have been simplified to our best ability, incorporating insights from a team of test diners and fellow cooks, with you—the Reader—as the 'Instant Chef' in the title ever in mind.

This is not a exhaustive guide but rather a personal exploration of traditions and experiments that have intellectually, socially, or emotionally resonated with me. It could have easily taken four different forms, with four unique sets of recipes. I sincerely hope you discover joy, secrets, laughter, and inspiration within the 180 recipes, with variations, that constitute this unique journal. I have endeavored to surprise and delight with each one.

Happy Cooking!
— Andrew West

Leonardo da Vinci:
"Simplicity is the ultimate sophistication."

Antoine de Saint-Exupéry:
"Perfection is achieved, not when there is nothing more to add, but when there is nothing left to take away."

Steve Jobs: "Simple can be harder than complex: You have to work hard to get your thinking clean to make it simple. But it's worth it in the end because once you get there, you can move mountains."

Julia Child: "You don't have to cook fancy or complicated masterpieces—just good food from fresh ingredients."

Author's Notes

There are three advanced techniques you will need to understand to get through all of the recipes in this book:

Making a Roux:
- Explanation: Melt 1/2 cup butter in a pan. Gradually whisk in 1/2 cup flour over low heat. Stir constantly for 5-10 mins until it turns golden. Adjust heat for desired color.

- Practical Application: Use in gumbo by adding vegetables, meats, and liquids to create a rich, flavorful base. For béchamel, whisk roux into warm milk for a creamy sauce.

Clarification of Stock:
- Explanation: Simmer 4 cups of stock. Whisk 2 egg whites until frothy; mix into stock. Allow to simmer without stirring for 15 mins. Strain through cheesecloth.

- Practical Application: Clarified stock enhances consommés and soups. For a clear broth, strain cooled stock through a fine mesh or cheesecloth, ensuring a pristine liquid.

Blanching Vegetables:
- Explanation: Bring a pot of water to boil. Submerge veggies asparagus, green beans) for 1-2 mins. Quickly transfer to ice water to halt cooking.

- Practical Application: Use blanched veggies for salads or stir-fries. Preserve bright colors and crisp textures. Blanching prepares vegetables for further cooking or freezing.

There are three books you need to read to make this Book more interesting:

James Beard's "American Cookery" (1972) is a culinary journey celebrating diverse American flavors. Beard, a gastronomic authority, intertwines recipes with historical insights. Focused on simplicity, the book demystifies cooking, making it a timeless classic for home cooks and a testament to Beard's passion for elevating American cuisine.

and

In "The Elements of Cooking," Michael Ruhlman, Nov. 6, 2007, the Author decodes chef expertise for all kitchens. A life-changing guide to culinary mastery.

and

The 1960s editions of "Joy of Cooking" maintained the iconic cookbook's tradition of comprehensive recipes with a focus on American home cooking. Revised by Irma S. Rombauer and Marion Rombauer Becker, these editions captured the culinary spirit of the decade.

THE INSTANT CHEF
AMERICAN CLASSICS
A HISTORY & COOKBOOK

ISBN
9781989647431

© 2024 Andrew West
A Byrd Press Publication
Toronto
www.byrdpress.com
publisher@byrdpress.com

Art Direction Avery Martin

THE INSTANT CHEF
AMERICAN CLASSICS
A HISTORY & COOKBOOK

I dedicate this Book to two people.
One who says, 'I haven't cooked that yet. I always wanted to try it…' and another who says 'why don't you include …'

THE INSTANT CHEF
AMERICAN CLASSICS
Table of Contents

Introduction to the American Eras...1

Colonial Era (1607-1776) ..6

Early Republic Era (1776-1846)...17

Antebellum Era (1846-1861)...27

Civil War Era (1861-1865)...37

Reconstruction Era (1865-1877)...46

Gilded Age (1877-1900) ...56

Progressive Era (1900-1920)...66

Roaring Twenties (1920-1929)...76

The Depression Era (1930s)

World War II Years (1940s)...102

The Post-War Boom (1950s)...112

The Gourmet Revolution (1960s)...123

The Me Generation (1970s)...134

The Reagan Era (1980s)...144

The Digital Age (1990s)...154

The New Millennium (2000s)...159

The Social Media Era (2010s)...166

The Atomized Era (2020s)...168

Final Thoughts...181

Index of Recipes by Page...182

Introduction to the American Eras

American cuisine, a captivating odyssey stretching from the Colonial (1607-1776) era to The Atomized Era (2020-), unveils a narrative woven with tradition, necessity, available ingredients, and the vibrant tapestry of cultural diversity that has shaped a culinary landscape standing the test of time. Each era, with its unique challenges and opportunities, has left an indelible mark on the nation's palate, reflecting the dynamic evolution of American culinary identity. While this is not a comprehensive encyclopedic of American cookery (they already exist) it is an idiosyncratic handbook that should provide a solid working overview of popular foods during different eras, foods that just about anyone with a set of very basic skills can master. With that in mind, let's take a quick look at the eras we will be touching upon in this Book.

Colonial Era (1607-1776):
In the early Colonial period, American cuisine was grounded in the principles of survival. Settlers, faced with a new and challenging environment, quickly learned from Native Americans how to utilize indigenous ingredients. Corn, beans, and squash became dietary staples, forming the foundation of Native American agriculture known as the "Three Sisters." As European settlers adapted, they introduced traditional European cooking methods and ingredients to the New World, creating a hybrid cuisine that laid the groundwork for the diverse culinary landscape that would unfold over centuries.

Early Republic Era (1776-1846):
The Early Republic Era witnessed the formation of a distinct American identity, and with it, a burgeoning culinary identity. The rejection of imported British goods during the Revolutionary era fostered a sense of self-reliance, prompting Americans to turn to locally available ingredients. Corn, now a staple, gave rise to cornbread and grits. As the nation expanded westward, regional variations in cuisine emerged, influenced by the availability of local produce and the culinary traditions of settlers.

Antebellum Era (1846-1861):
The Antebellum Era brought about a culinary landscape shaped by regional flavors and influences. Southern cuisine, characterized by soulful comfort foods, was born out of a fusion of African, European, and Indigenous culinary legacies. The use of corn, rice, and seafood in the South, alongside the influence of French and Spanish cooking techniques, resulted in iconic dishes like Pickled Watermelon Rind and Jambalaya.

Civil War Era (1861-1865):
The Civil War Era brought challenges that impacted the availability of ingredients and necessitated resourcefulness in the kitchen. Creative cooks adapted to limited resources, introducing dishes like corn dodgers and salted meats. The struggle for sustenance during these tumultuous years laid the groundwork for a tradition of hearty, preserved foods that would echo through subsequent eras.

Reconstruction Era (1865-1877):
Following the Civil War, the Reconstruction Era witnessed a period of rebuilding and resilience. Culinary traditions persisted and adapted to the changing times. The introduction of canned goods and processed foods began to influence American kitchens, offering convenience in an era of transformation.

Gilded Age (1877-1900):
The Gilded Age ushered in an era of economic growth, technological innovation, and culinary exploration. Advances in transportation and communication facilitated the exchange of culinary ideas across regions. The era embraced the concept of "high society" dining, with an emphasis on extravagant banquets and elaborate dishes.

Progressive Era (1900-1920)
During the Progressive Era (1900-1920), a wave of social reform extended to the culinary landscape, fostering a heightened awareness of food safety and healthful eating. The introduction of regulations coincided with a burgeoning interest in home economics, significantly influencing how Americans approached cooking and nutrition. This era witnessed not only a commitment to healthier dietary practices but also the rise of culinary innovations, such as the incorporation of dried chipped beef and the crafting of homemade ketchup, reflecting a dynamic period of both societal progress and evolving culinary tastes. The emphasis on safety and nutrition laid the foundation for a more conscious and experimental approach to food, showcasing the Progressive Era's lasting impact on the American culinary ethos.

Roaring Twenties (1920-1929):
The Roaring Twenties, a time of prosperity and cultural dynamism, saw a departure from the constraints of earlier decades. Prohibition led to the rise of speakeasies, and clandestine gatherings embraced creative cocktails and decadent dishes. The era's culinary landscape reflected a newfound exuberance and experimentation.

The Depression Era (1930s):
The Great Depression challenged Americans to create nourishing meals with limited resources. "Depression-era" recipes like meatloaf, casseroles, and

macaroni and cheese emerged, reflecting an era of frugality and resourcefulness that still resonates in modern comfort food.

World War II Years (1940s):
World War II introduced rationing, prompting cooks to innovate with available ingredients. Postwar prosperity brought convenience foods, with diners and canned goods becoming emblematic of the era. In fact, in the 1940s, diners proliferated across the U.S., becoming iconic symbols of American dining culture. These casual eateries, marked by their retro aesthetics and affordable menus, emerged as popular gathering spots, reflecting a societal shift towards more accessible and informal dining experiences during this era. Meanwhile, the rise of fast food chains laid the groundwork for a global influence on American tastes.

The Post-War Boom (1950s):
The post-war boom of the 1950s witnessed a shift towards convenience and mass production. Convenience foods like TV Dinners and comforting ethnic foods, like the Cuban sandwich, became popular, reflecting the era's emphasis on efficiency and a desire for novelty and reliability.

The Gourmet Revolution (1960s):
The 1960s marked a culinary renaissance with a renewed interest in fresh, locally sourced ingredients. The rise of culinary luminaries like Julia Child and the emergence of California cuisine celebrated diverse flavors and elevated the status of chefs in American culture.

The Me Generation (1970s):
The 1970s saw a continued focus on fresh and natural foods. A counter-cultural movement led to an increased interest in vegetarianism, and health-conscious eating gained popularity.

The Reagan Era (1980s):
The 1980s witnessed the influence of the Reagan era on American dining. Fast food culture proliferated, and the decade embraced excess with extravagant dishes and indulgent desserts.

The Digital Age (1990s):
The 1990s brought the rise of the digital age, transforming the way people accessed information, including recipes. The culinary landscape began to globalize further, with an increased interest in international cuisines and ingredients.

The New Millennium (2000s):
The 21st century witnessed a resurgence of interest in locally sourced, sustainable ingredients. The farm-to-table movement championed by chefs and

consumers alike emphasized the importance of knowing where food comes from, reconnecting with seasonal produce, and supporting local farmers.

The Social Media Era (2010s):
The 2010s marked the advent of the Social Media Era, where food became a visual and shareable experience. Food blogging, Instagram, and other platforms transformed the way people discovered, shared, and engaged with recipes.

The Atomized Era (2020-):
As we enter Atomized Era, where everything seems to be breaking apart and reconnecting in new ways, there's a continued celebration of diverse influences and culinary creativity. This era embraces the rich tapestry of flavors that make up American cuisine, acknowledging the significance of tradition, the availability of ingredients, and the ongoing dialogue between cultures that shape our culinary identity. It is an era characterized by a deep appreciation for the artistry and romance inherent in the culture of foods and ingredients from around the world and across the bridge of time and tradition. For a person that loves food history, food science, food culture and playing in the kitchen, it is a good time to continue cooking.

THE INSTANT CHEF
AMERICAN CLASSICS
THE RECIPES

Colonial Era (1607-1776)

Shellfish and Sea Vegetable Three Sisters Stew

The Shellfish and Sea Veg Three Sisters Stew marries Native American agricultural traditions with colonial coastal living during the historical period. The Three Sisters—corn, beans, and squash—represent a sustainable farming approach, while shellfish and sea vegetables showcase coastal abundance. Coastal regions offered clams and mussels as staple proteins, preserved through salting or smoking. Native American tribes harvested sea vegetables like seaweed. This culinary fusion symbolizes the interconnectedness of cultures, as these diverse ingredients were adapted across communities. The stew likely simmered in large pots over open fires, embodying a blend of foraged, farmed, and preserved elements. This dish not only reflects historical ingredient availability but also illustrates the cultural exchange and adaptability present in colonial-era cuisine.

Ingredients

- Corn kernels
- Black beans
- Cubed butternut squash
- Clams or mussels
- Seaweed (such as dulse or kelp), rehydrated if dried
- Vegetable or seafood broth
- Onion, garlic, and bell peppers
- Thyme, smoked paprika, salt, and pepper
- Olive oil or salted pork fat for flavor

Instructions

1. Sauté chopped onions, garlic, and bell peppers in olive oil or salted pork fat until softened.

2. Add corn, black beans, and cubed butternut squash to the pot; stir and cook briefly.

3. Pour in vegetable or seafood broth, bring the mixture to a simmer.

4. Season with thyme, smoked paprika, salt, and pepper according to taste.

5. Once butternut squash is almost tender, introduce clams or mussels to the pot.

6. Cover and simmer until the shellfish open and are cooked.

7. Finally, add rehydrated sea vegetables to the stew; adjust seasoning if necessary.

8. Serve hot, ensuring each bowl contains a mix of the Three Sisters (corn, beans, squash), shellfish, and sea vegetables.

Colonial Era (1607-1776)

Johnnycakes

Johnnycakes, also known as journey cakes or johnnycorn cakes, have a rich history dating back to the indigenous peoples of North America. Made from a mixture of cornmeal, water, and sometimes salt, these simple flatbreads were introduced to European settlers by Native Americans, who then adapted the recipe with local ingredients.

During the colonial era, johnnycakes became a household staple in America, especially in the Southern and New England regions. Easy to make and providing a hearty meal, these cakes gained popularity for their simplicity. Over time, regional variations emerged, with some areas incorporating wheat flour or adding milk and leavening agents to the recipe. This culinary evolution showcases the adaptability of johnnycakes, blending indigenous traditions with the influences of European settlers, contributing to the diverse tapestry of American cuisine.

Ingredients

- 1 cup cornmeal
- 1 cup all-purpose flour
- 1 tablespoon sugar
- 1 teaspoon baking powder
- 1/2 teaspoon salt
- 1 cup milk
- 1/4 cup melted butter

Instructions

1. In a bowl, mix 1 cup each of cornmeal and flour, 1 tbsp sugar, 1 tsp baking powder, 1/2 tsp salt.

2. Add 1 cup milk, 1/4 cup melted butter. Stir, ladle onto a buttered griddle.

3. Cook until golden. Drizzle with syrup.

For Rosemary Brown Butter

Ingredients:

- Butter
- Fresh rosemary
- Sea salt

Instructions:

1. Brown butter in a pan, adding fresh rosemary.

2. Allow the rosemary to infuse; strain it out.

3. Sprinkle with sea salt and drizzle the aromatic brown butter over Johnny Cakes.

Colonial Era (1607-1776)

Ash Cake

Ash cakes, rooted in Native American and colonial cooking, are typically made with cornmeal, water, and salt, shaped into flat cakes, and baked directly in ashes or on a heated surface like a hoe. Johnnycakes, another type of cornmeal-based flatbread, may include additional ingredients like milk and butter, and are cooked on a griddle without the association with ashes. While both share historical ties, ash cakes are more specifically linked to a particular cooking method and cultural history.

Ash cake, or hoe cake, symbolizes early settlers' resourcefulness with basic ingredients like cornmeal, water, and salt. Baked in ashes or on a heated surface, it reflects the fusion of indigenous and colonial culinary practices, contributing to distinct American cuisine. Its enduring simplicity serves as a flavorful link to the past, encapsulating shared history and diverse heritage.

Ingredients

- 2 cups cornmeal
- 1 teaspoon salt (optional)
- Water (approximately 1 to 1.5 cups, or as needed to form a dough)

Instructions

1. Mix 2 cups cornmeal with water (1-1.5 cups) to form a dough. Optionally, add 1 tsp salt. Shape into flat cakes.

2. Cook directly on hot ashes or a heated surface like a hoe.

For Berry Compote with Lavender:

Ingredients:

- Mixed berries (strawberries, blueberries, raspberries)
- Sugar
- Lavender buds (dried or fresh)

Instructions:

1. Cook berries with sugar until they release juices.

2. Stir in lavender buds and let it simmer.

3. Serve the aromatic compote over Ash Cakes.

Colonial Era (1607-1776)

Hoecakes- Refined Version

Johnnycakes, ash cakes, and hoecakes are traditional flatbreads with distinct characteristics. Johnnycakes, typically made with cornmeal, water, and salt, are cooked on a griddle and hold variations like Rhode Island johnnycakes. Ash cakes, comprising basic ingredients like cornmeal, water, and salt, are shaped and baked directly in ashes or on a heated surface. Hoecakes, also made from cornmeal, water, and salt, derive their name from being cooked on a garden hoe or griddle over an open flame. Unlike johnnycakes and ash cakes, hoecakes evolved regionally, symbolizing resourcefulness for pioneers. Each type reflects unique ingredients, preparation methods, and cultural associations in early American culinary traditions. Our recipe is a reflection of how the basic recipe can be adapted and refined.

Ingredients

- 1 cup cornmeal
- 1/2 cup all-purpose flour
- 1 tablespoon sugar
- 1 teaspoon baking powder
- 1/2 teaspoon salt
- 1 cup buttermilk
- 1 large egg
- 2 tablespoons melted butter
- 1/2 teaspoon vanilla extract (optional)
- Cooking oil or butter for greasing the griddle

Instructions

1. Simmer 1 lb cleaned tripe, onion, carrots, potatoes, bell pepper, and garlic in 4 cups beef broth. Add bay leaf, salt, and pepper; simmer for 2-3 hours.

2. Adjust seasoning and, if desired, add hot peppers for extra spice.

For Cider Reduction Glaze:

Ingredients:
- Apple cider
- Brown sugar
- Cinnamon

Instructions:

1. Simmer apple cider, brown sugar, and cinnamon until reduced to a glaze.

2. Spoon over Hoe Cakes for a sweet and spiced flavor.

Colonial Era (1607-1776)

Clam Chowder

American clam chowder has deep roots in New England, particularly along the coastal areas of Massachusetts, dating back to the early 18th century. French and British settlers introduced their soup and stew traditions to the American colonies, shaping the foundation of this iconic dish.

The earliest written clam chowder recipe, documented in the Boston Evening Post in 1751, marked a pivotal moment in the dish's history. Traditional New England clam chowder typically includes clams, salt pork, onions, and potatoes simmered in a milk or cream-based broth. Over time, regional variations emerged, with preferences for either a clear broth or a thicker, roux-based consistency, showcasing the adaptability and diverse influences that have enriched American culinary traditions.

Ingredients

- 4 slices bacon, diced
- 1 onion, finely chopped
- 2 celery stalks, diced
- 3 potatoes, peeled and diced
- 2 cups clam juice
- 3 cups chopped clams (fresh or canned)
- 2 cups whole milk
- 1 cup heavy cream
- 3 tablespoons all-purpose flour
- 2 bay leaves
- Salt and pepper to taste
- Fresh parsley, chopped, for garnish

Instructions

1. Sizzle bacon. Add onions, celery, potatoes.
2. Pour in clam juice, clams, milk, cream. Whisk in flour. Toss in bay leaves. Season.
3. Simmer to perfection.
4. Garnish with parsley.

Variation
Bacon and Leek Clam Chowder:

Replace onions with leeks for a milder flavor. Infuse a smoky essence by using smoked bacon. Finish with a sprinkle of grated Parmesan.

Colonial Era (1607-1776)

Pepper Pot Soup

Pepper Pot Soup, also known as Philadelphia Pepper Pot, has its roots in 18th-century America, particularly during the Revolutionary War. Legend has it that at Valley Forge in 1777-1778, facing food shortages, cooks created this hearty soup by combining tripe, vegetables, and spicy peppers, providing warmth and sustenance to the Continental Army. Inspired by Afro-Caribbean Ajiaco, Pepper Pot Soup symbolizes resourcefulness and remains a flavorful reminder of historical challenges and culinary innovation in the United States. You can use pork shoulder, trimmed of fat and cubed, or dark meat chicken if shy of tripe. Pork shoulder has good marbling and can add richness to the soup, while using dark chicken meat, such as thighs or drumsticks, in the Pepper Pot Soup can add richness and depth of flavor to the broth. Dark meat has a higher fat content compared to white meat, which contributes to a more savory and flavorful soup.

Ingredients

- 1 lb tripe, cleaned and sliced
- 1 onion, chopped
- 2 carrots, diced
- 2 potatoes, diced
- 1 bell pepper, chopped
- 2 cloves garlic, minced
- 4 cups beef broth
- 1 cup water
- 1 bay leaf
- Salt and pepper to taste
- Hot peppers (optional, for spice- Cubanelle or Sweet Banana for milder heat, Scotch Bonnet for serious heat)

Instructions

1. Simmer 1 lb cleaned tripe, onion, carrots, potatoes, bell pepper, and garlic in 4 cups beef broth. Add bay leaf, salt, and pepper.

2. Simmer for 2-3 hours.

3. Adjust seasoning and, if desired, add hot peppers for extra spice.

Variation
Hard Cider and Apple Tripe Stew:

Replace a portion of the water with hard cider, a beverage that was popular during the colonial period. Add diced apples towards the end of the cooking process to bring in a touch of sweetness and acidity, providing a unique colonial twist to the dish.

Colonial Era (1607-1776)

Apple Tansey

Apple Tansey, an enduring English dessert rooted in history, traces its origins to the medieval era and flourished in popularity during the 17th and 18th centuries. The term "tansey," harkening back to Old French and Middle English, broadly denotes a dish featuring eggs. The classic Apple Tansey recipe involves the artful combination of sliced apples immersed in a sweetened egg batter, resulting in a sumptuous custard-like texture. A final touch sees the mixture skillfully pan-fried to a golden brown perfection.

Throughout its evolution, this time-honored dish has embraced variations, incorporating elements such as sugar, cinnamon, and nutmeg to enhance its flavor profile. Apple Tansey stands as a delightful embodiment of English culinary heritage, captivating palates with its enduring charm and classic appeal.

Ingredients

- 2 apples, thinly sliced
- 4 tablespoons butter
- 2 tablespoons sugar
- 3 eggs
- 1/4 cup milk
- 1/2 cup flour
- 1/4 teaspoon nutmeg
- 1/4 teaspoon cinnamon
- Pinch of salt

Instructions

1. Sauté apples in 2 tbsp butter and 1 tbsp sugar until golden.

2. Whisk eggs, milk, flour, nutmeg, cinnamon, and a pinch of salt in a bowl.

3. Pour batter over apples in the pan, cook until set, then flip.

4. Add 2 tbsp butter and 1 tbsp sugar, cook until caramelized.

Variation
Dried Fruit and Citrus Zest Infusion:

Add 1/4 cup chopped dried fruit (raisins/currants) and zest of half a lemon or orange into the batter elevate the colonial-inspired apple tansey.

Colonial Era (1607-1776)

Asparagus and Hazelnut Succotash

Traditional succotash, rooted in Native American and colonial cuisine, combines lima beans, corn, and other seasonal vegetables. Our elevated "Asparagus and Hazelnut Succotash" pays homage to this classic, introducing asparagus, hazelnuts, and contemporary flavors. As we evolve this staple, we celebrate the historical fusion of indigenous and colonial culinary traditions. The addition of asparagus brings a vibrant, crisp texture, while hazelnuts contribute a rich, nutty undertone. This variation aims to offer a modern twist, engaging in a conversation with colonial menus by embracing ingredients available during that era while adapting to evolving tastes. The goal is to elevate the succotash experience, maintaining its cultural ties while inviting exploration and dialogue around the dynamic evolution of American culinary heritage.

Ingredients

- Asparagus, cut into bite-sized pieces
- Fresh corn kernels
- Butter beans
- Cherry tomatoes, halved
- Toasted hazelnuts, chopped
- Fresh basil, chiffonade
- Balsamic glaze
- Salt and pepper to taste

Instructions

1. Sauté asparagus until slightly tender.

2. Add corn, butter beans, and cherry tomatoes.

3. Stir in toasted hazelnuts and fresh basil.

4. Drizzle with balsamic glaze; season with salt and pepper.

Colonial Era (1607-1776)

Pemmican (Native American influence)

Pemmican, a venerable component of North American indigenous cuisine, traces its roots to the Great Plains, particularly among Native peoples. Crafted from dried and pounded meat, often sourced from bison or deer, mixed with rendered fat and occasionally dried berries, pemmican takes the form of convenient cakes or bars. This traditional fare served as a portable, non-perishable, and highly nutritious sustenance, proving crucial for nomadic communities facing scarcity or undertaking extensive journeys.

Symbolizing resourcefulness, pemmican stands as a historical testament to the adaptive ingenuity of indigenous peoples in utilizing available resources. Its enduring significance lies in its representation of traditional indigenous foodways, highlighting the intersection of culinary artistry, practicality, and the deep connection between food and survival within these communities.

Ingredients

- Lean meat (such as bison, deer, or beef)
- Rendered fat (often from the same animal as the meat)
- Dried berries (optional, for flavor and additional nutrition)

Instructions

1. Dry and pound lean meat (bison, deer) into a powder.

2. Mix the meat powder with an equal amount of rendered fat.

3. Optionally, include dried berries for taste.

4. Form the mixture into cakes or bars.

Variation
Add 1-2 cloves minced garlic and 1-2 tsp dried rosemary for robust Rosemary and Garlic Pemmican

Colonial Era (1607-1776)

Hasty Pudding

Hasty Pudding, originating in the 17th century, is a traditional English and American dish known for its simplicity and quick preparation. Typically made with ingredients like wheat flour or cornmeal, milk or water, and sweeteners, it symbolizes early colonial culinary practices. Over time, regional adaptations and variations emerged, highlighting its enduring cultural significance.

In the United States, Hasty Pudding took on an additional cultural dimension with the annual "Hasty Pudding Show" at Harvard University. This theatrical production, ongoing since the late 18th century, adds a lighthearted and humorous element to the historical culinary term, showcasing its lasting impact on both traditional recipes and entertainment.

Ingredients

- 1 cup cornmeal
- 4 cups milk
- 1/4 cup sugar
- Pinch of salt
- Optional: molasses or sweetener of choice

Instructions

1. In a pot, combine cornmeal, milk, sugar, and salt.

2. Over medium heat, cook the mixture, stirring constantly until it thickens.

3. Adjust sweetness to taste by adding an optional sweetener.

4. Once thickened, serve the warm mixture for a quick and comforting treat.

Variation
Vanilla Bean and Berries Hasty Pudding:

Infuse the milk with a split vanilla bean during heating. Top with fresh berries or a berry compote before serving, adding a burst of fruity sweetness.

Colonial Era (1607-1776)

New England Boiled Dinner

New England Boiled Dinner, rooted in colonial practices dating to the 18th century, holds an enduring place in American cuisine. Originating from the practical method of boiling meats and vegetables together, this robust dish reflects the resourcefulness of early settlers. Its evolution over time has transformed it into a showcase, featuring corned beef or ham as the centerpiece, accompanied by a harmonious medley of cabbage, potatoes, carrots, and turnips. The resulting amalgamation offers a flavorful and wholesome meal that not only gratifies the palate but also stands as a testament to the lasting legacy of colonial culinary practices. New England Boiled Dinner is a symbol of culinary heritage, encapsulating the simplicity and richness that define the gastronomic traditions of the region.

Ingredients

- 3 lbs corned beef or ham
- 4 potatoes, quartered
- 4 carrots, chopped
- 1 cabbage, cut into wedges
- 3 turnips, peeled and diced
- Salt and pepper to taste

Instructions

1. Simmer 3 lbs corned beef or ham in water for 2 hours.

2. Add 4 potatoes, 4 carrots, 3 turnips, salt, and pepper; simmer for an additional 30-45 minutes.

3. Add cabbage wedges and simmer for an additional 15-20 minutes.

4. Serve hot, slicing the meat and arranging the vegetables.

Variation
Mustard and Brown Sugar Glaze:

Mix Dijon mustard and brown sugar to create a glaze for the corned beef. Apply during the final cooking stage for a tangy and caramelized finish

Early Republic Era (1776-1846)

Brunswick Stew

Brunswick Stew, a beloved Southern culinary treasure, traces its origins to the 19th century, sparking debates over whether Virginia or Georgia claims its true birthplace. Legend intertwines with history, suggesting that the stew emerged from communal efforts during a spirited hunting party in Brunswick County, Virginia. This Southern delicacy seamlessly melded local game with tomatoes, corn, and an assortment of vegetables. Regardless of the exact birthplace, Brunswick Stew has entrenched itself as a quintessential Southern dish, celebrated for its rich flavors and cultural significance in communal gatherings and family events. The amalgamation of regional ingredients mirrors the diverse culinary landscape of the South, solidifying Brunswick Stew's status as not just a savory delight but a symbol of shared heritage and communal joy.

Ingredients

- 1 whole chicken, cooked and shredded (or 3-4 cups cooked chicken meat)
- 1 pound smoked pork or ham, diced
- 1 large onion, finely chopped
- 3 cloves garlic, minced
- 2 cups lima beans, frozen or fresh
- 2 cups corn kernels, fresh or frozen
- 2 cups diced tomatoes (canned or fresh)
- 1 cup tomato sauce
- 1 cup barbecue sauce
- 1 teaspoon hot sauce (adjust to taste)
- Salt and pepper to taste
- Chicken broth or water as needed
- Optional: 1 cup okra, sliced (for a traditional touch)

Instructions

1. Cook and shred 1 whole chicken.

2. In a pot, combine chicken, diced smoked pork/ham, onion, garlic, lima beans, corn, diced tomatoes, tomato sauce, and barbecue sauce.

3. Add hot sauce, salt, and pepper to taste.

4. Simmer until flavors meld, adding broth/water as needed.

5. Optional: add sliced okra for a traditional touch.

Early Republic Era (1776-1846)

Chicken Pot Pie

The history of American chicken pot pie is deeply intertwined with European culinary traditions and the adaptation of recipes by early American settlers. Originating from the medieval British practice of enclosing meats in pastry, pot pies were brought to America by European colonists. The American version evolved to showcase locally available ingredients, with chicken becoming a popular choice. By the 19th century, chicken pot pie had firmly established itself as a comforting and hearty dish, often associated with home-cooked meals and family gatherings. Today, it remains a cherished part of American cuisine, with regional variations reflecting diverse culinary influences and preferences across the United States.

Ingredients

- 2 cups cooked and shredded chicken (rotisserie or roasted)
- 2 tablespoons olive oil
- 1 cup diced onion
- 1 cup diced carrots
- 1 cup diced celery
- 2 cloves garlic, minced
- 1/2 cup frozen peas
- 1/2 cup frozen corn
- 1/4 cup all-purpose flour
- 2 cups chicken broth
- 1 cup whole milk
- 1 teaspoon dried thyme
- Salt and pepper to taste
- 1/4 cup fresh parsley, chopped
- Pre-made or homemade pie crust (for top and bottom)

Instructions

1. Sauté onions, carrots, celery, and garlic in olive oil.

2. Add shredded chicken, peas, corn, and flour.

3. Pour in chicken broth, milk, and thyme.

4. Season with salt and pepper.

5. Simmer until thickened.

6. Stir in fresh parsley.

7. Line a pie dish with crust, add the filling, top with another crust.

8. Bake at 375°F (190°C) for approximately 25-30 minutes or until golden.

Early Republic Era (1776-1846)

Cornbread

American cornbread has a rich history deeply intertwined with the indigenous peoples and early settlers of North America. Native Americans, including the Cherokee and Creek tribes, were early practitioners of using ground maize to create a simple form of cornbread. As European settlers arrived, they adopted and adapted these techniques, incorporating cornmeal into their diets. Cornbread became a staple in the Southern United States, where corn thrived in the warm climate. The versatility of cornbread allowed for various regional adaptations, from skillet-baked versions to sweeter renditions with added ingredients like molasses. Today, American cornbread remains a beloved side dish, symbolizing the fusion of Native American and European culinary traditions.

Ingredients

- 1 cup cornmeal
- 1 cup all-purpose flour
- 1/4 cup sugar
- 1 tablespoon baking powder
- 1/2 teaspoon baking soda
- 1/2 teaspoon salt
- 1 cup buttermilk
- 1/2 cup unsalted butter, melted
- 2 large eggs
- 1 cup fresh or frozen corn kernels
- 1/4 cup chopped fresh herbs (such as chives or parsley)
- 1 cup shredded cheese (cheddar or pepper jack for a kick)

Instructions

1. Mix 1 cup cornmeal, 1 cup flour, 1/4 cup sugar, baking powder, baking soda, and salt.

2. In a separate bowl, whisk buttermilk, melted butter, and eggs.

3. Combine wet and dry ingredients.

4. Fold in corn, herbs, and shredded cheese.

5. Pour into a greased baking dish.

6. Bake at 375°F (190°C) for approximately 25-30 minutes or until golden.

Early Republic Era (1776-1846)

Shoo Fly Pie

Shoo Fly Pie is a traditional American dessert with roots in the Pennsylvania Dutch and Amish communities. Originating in the 19th century, this molasses-based pie is renowned for its distinctive sweet and gooey filling. The name "Shoo Fly Pie" is said to have originated from the need to shoo away flies attracted to the molasses sweetness. The pie typically consists of a crumbly, streusel-like topping made with flour, brown sugar, and butter, covering a rich molasses and sometimes sorghum or dark syrup filling. Shoo Fly Pie represents a delicious intersection of simple, pantry-staple ingredients and the culinary traditions of the Pennsylvania Dutch, making it a beloved treat with a unique history.

Ingredients

For the Crumb Topping:
- 1 1/2 cups all-purpose flour
- 1 cup brown sugar
- 2 tablespoons butter

For the Molasses Filling:
- 1 cup molasses
- 3/4 cup hot water
- 1/2 teaspoon baking soda

For the Pie Shell:
- 1 unbaked pie crust

Instructions

1. Mix 1.5 cups flour, 1 cup brown sugar, and 2 tbsp butter for the crumbly topping.

2. For the filling, combine 1 cup molasses, 3/4 cup hot water, and 1/2 tsp baking soda.

3. Pour into an unbaked pie crust, then sprinkle the crumbly topping.

4. Bake at 375°F for 40-45 mins until set.

Early Republic Era (1776-1846)

Gumbo

Gumbo, a staple of Louisiana cuisine, boasts a rich history shaped by diverse cultural influences. Rooted in West African, French, Spanish, and Native American culinary traditions, gumbo's evolution embodies the melting pot of Louisiana's Creole and Cajun cultures. The name itself is believed to have West African origins, with "ki ngombo" signifying okra, a key ingredient. Gumbo typically features a roux, okra, or filé powder, combined with a variety of proteins like seafood, chicken, and sausage. As a symbol of Louisiana's cultural amalgamation, gumbo reflects the region's dynamic history, making it a flavorful embodiment of its diverse culinary heritage.

Ingredients

- 1 cup all-purpose flour
- 1 cup vegetable oil or unsalted butter (for making a roux)
- 1 large onion, finely diced
- 1 bell pepper, finely diced
- 2 celery stalks, finely diced
- 4 cloves garlic, minced
- 1 pound andouille sausage, sliced
- 1 pound chicken thighs, diced
- 1 pound shrimp, peeled and deveined
- 1 cup okra, sliced
- 1 can (28 ounces) diced tomatoes
- 8 cups chicken or seafood broth
- 2 bay leaves
- 1 teaspoon dried thyme or filé powder
- 1 teaspoon smoked paprika
- 1 teaspoon cayenne pepper (adjust to taste)
- Salt and black pepper to taste
- Fresh parsley and green onions for garnish

Instructions

1. Whisk 1 cup flour with 1 cup oil/butter until dark brown for a roux.

2. Sauté onion, bell pepper, celery, garlic, and andouille sausage.

3. Add diced chicken, shrimp, and okra.

4. Pour in diced tomatoes, broth, bay leaves, thyme, smoked paprika, cayenne, salt, and pepper.

5. Simmer until flavors meld.

6. Serve over rice, garnish with fresh parsley and green onions.

Early Republic Era (1776-1846)

Sally Lunn Buns

Sally Lunn Buns, a beloved British culinary tradition, trace their history to the 17th century. The name is often linked to a young Frenchwoman, possibly named Solange Luyon, who settled in Bath, England, and started selling a delicate, enriched bread. Sally Lunn's buns quickly gained popularity for their light, brioche-like texture and slightly sweet taste. Over the centuries, these buns evolved, becoming a staple in British tea culture. Today, Sally Lunn Buns are cherished as a versatile treat, enjoyed both sweet with jams and savory as a base for various toppings, embodying a timeless legacy of delicious simplicity in British baking.

Ingredients

- 4 cups all-purpose flour
- 1/4 cup sugar
- 2 teaspoons active dry yeast
- 1 cup warm milk
- 1/2 cup unsalted butter, melted
- 3 large eggs
- 1/2 teaspoon salt
Additional flour for kneading (if needed)

Some variations of Sally Lunn Buns may include additional ingredients like lemon zest or currants for added flavor.

Instructions

1. Dissolve 2 tsp yeast in 1 cup warm milk.

2. In a bowl, combine 4 cups flour, 1/4 cup sugar, and 1/2 tsp salt.

3. Add yeast mixture, melted butter, and 3 eggs. Mix until a soft dough forms.

4. Knead on a floured surface until smooth.

5. Place in a greased bowl, cover, and let rise until doubled.

6. Punch down and shape into buns.

7. Place in a buttered pan, let rise again.

8. Bake at 375°F until golden- approx 15-20 minutes.

Early Republic Era (1776-1846)

Spoonbread

Spoonbread, a classic Southern dish, has roots in Native American and African American culinary traditions. Native Americans introduced corn-based dishes, and African Americans later incorporated the idea into their cooking. The name "spoonbread" reflects its unique texture, as it's softer than cornbread but denser than grits or corn pudding. Typically made with cornmeal, milk, eggs, and leavening agents, spoonbread is baked to a pudding-like consistency. It gained popularity in the South during the 19th century and remains a comforting and versatile dish. Spoonbread's legacy lies in its ability to adapt, making it a timeless representation of Southern culinary heritage. This version is an elevated variation on the historic recipe.

Ingredients

- 1 cup cornmeal
- 1 cup all-purpose flour
- 1/2 cup unsalted butter, melted
- 1/2 cup honey or maple syrup
- 4 cups whole milk
- 4 large eggs
- 1 teaspoon baking powder
- 1/2 teaspoon salt

Instructions

1. Mix cornmeal, flour, melted butter, honey, warm milk, eggs, baking powder, and salt.

2. Bake in a preheated oven at 375°F (190°C) until golden and gooey, about 45 minutes.

For Classic Caramelized Onion Gravy:
Caramelize onions in butter, whisk in flour, and pour in broth for a classic caramelized onion gravy. Season with salt and pepper.

Early Republic Era (1776-1846)

(Mock) Terrapin Soup

Terrapin soup, a delicacy in American culinary history, gained prominence in the 19th century. The diamondback terrapin, a species of turtle found in coastal areas, was a sought-after ingredient for its flavorful and tender meat. Native American and African American culinary influences, particularly in the Chesapeake Bay region, contributed to its popularity. Terrapin soup became synonymous with luxury and was enjoyed by affluent diners in elite restaurants. However, overharvesting and conservation concerns led to a decline in terrapin populations. While less common today, terrapin soup remains a fascinating chapter in America's gastronomic past, highlighting the intersection of cultures and changing culinary trends. We are using wild game meats, here, to replace the terrapin, this allows you to create a complex and interesting flavor profile.

Ingredients

- 1 pound wild game meat (venison, elk, buffalo or a mix), diced
- 4 cups beef or game broth
- 1/4 cup unsalted butter
- 1/4 cup all-purpose flour
- 1 cup diced onion
- 1 cup diced celery
- 1 cup diced carrots
- 3 cloves garlic, minced
- 1/2 cup dry sherry or white wine (optional)
- 1 teaspoon Worcestershire sauce
- 1 bay leaf
- 1/2 teaspoon dried thyme
- Salt and black pepper to taste
- 1/4 cup heavy cream
- Chopped fresh parsley for garnish

Instructions

1. Sauté diced wild game meat in butter. Set aside.

2. Sauté onions, celery, carrots, and garlic. Sprinkle flour, create a roux.

3. Gradually add broth, return meat.

4. Stir in sherry, Worcestershire, bay leaf, thyme, salt, and pepper.

5. Simmer 30-40 mins.

6. Just before serving, add heavy cream. Garnish with parsley.

Early Republic Era (1776-1846)

Apple Pandowdy

Apple Pandowdy, a comforting dessert in American cuisine, traces its roots to colonial times. Originating from British predecessors, this rustic dish gained popularity for its simplicity and deliciousness. Typically made with sliced apples, sugar, and spices, the filling is covered with a buttery, biscuit-like crust. What sets Pandowdy apart is its unique preparation—after baking, the crust is broken into pieces and pressed into the bubbling fruit, creating a charmingly messy appearance. Served warm with a scoop of vanilla ice cream, Apple Pandowdy embodies the wholesome flavors of American home baking, offering a timeless and delightful treat that has endured through generations. Top with ice cream for a more decadent treat!

Ingredients

For the Filling:
- 6-8 cups apples, peeled, cored, and sliced (a mix of tart and sweet varieties)
- 1/2 to 3/4 cup granulated sugar (adjust based on sweetness preference)
- 1 teaspoon ground cinnamon
- 1/4 teaspoon ground nutmeg
- 2 tablespoons all-purpose flour
- 1 tablespoon lemon juice

For the Crust:
- 2 cups all-purpose flour
- 1/4 cup granulated sugar
- 1 tablespoon baking powder
- 1/2 teaspoon salt
- 3/4 cup unsalted butter, cold and cubed
- 2/3 cup whole milk

Instructions

1. Mix sliced apples with sugar, cinnamon, nutmeg, flour, and lemon juice.

2. Spread in a baking dish.

3. For the crust, combine flour, sugar, baking powder, salt, and cold butter until crumbly.

4. Add milk, form a dough.

5. Drop spoonfuls on the apples.

6. Bake until golden and bubbly.

7. Now comes the fun part—break the crust into the apples!

8. Serve warm.

Early Republic Era (1776-1846)

Hoppin' John

Hoppin' John, a quintessential American dish, boasts a history rooted in Southern culinary traditions. Originating during the antebellum era, it was a staple among African American communities in the South. Consisting of black-eyed peas, rice, and pork, the dish symbolized prosperity and good luck, with the peas representing coins. Its name likely evolved from the phrase "hop-in' John" or the ritual of "hopping" around the table before consuming the meal. Today, Hoppin' John remains a cherished New Year's tradition, embodying the rich cultural tapestry of the American South and celebrating the resilience and creativity of its diverse culinary heritage.

Ingredients

- 4 cups chicken or vegetable broth
- 1 onion, finely chopped
- 1 bell pepper, diced
- 2 celery stalks, diced
- 3 cloves garlic, minced
- 1 bay leaf
- 1 teaspoon dried thyme
- 1 teaspoon smoked paprika
- 1/2 teaspoon cayenne pepper (adjust to taste)
- Salt and black pepper to taste
- 1 ham hock or 1 cup diced ham
- Green onions and fresh parsley for garnish

Instructions

1. Soak black-eyed peas overnight.

2. Sauté onion, bell pepper, celery, and garlic.

3. Add drained peas, rice, broth, bay leaf, thyme, smoked paprika, cayenne, salt, pepper, and ham hock.

4. Bring to a boil, then simmer until peas are tender.

5. Remove ham hock, shred meat, and return to the pot.

6. Serve over rice, garnish with green onions and parsley. Serve with hot sauce on the side.

Antebellum Era (1846-1861)

Southern Biscuits and Gravy

Southern Biscuits and Gravy, a beloved comfort dish in American cuisine, has roots in Southern culinary traditions. Emerging in the 19th century, it combines the English influence of biscuits with the frugality of using leftover pork gravy. As settlers adapted to the ingredients available in the South, the dish evolved to feature soft, flaky biscuits smothered in a creamy and peppery sausage gravy. Its affordability and hearty nature made it a staple, especially during challenging times. Today, Southern Biscuits and Gravy remains a cherished breakfast or brunch classic, embodying the warmth and simplicity of Southern comfort food.

Ingredients

For the Biscuits:
- 2 cups all-purpose flour
- 1 tablespoon baking powder
- 1/2 teaspoon baking soda
- 1/2 teaspoon salt
- 1/2 cup unsalted butter, cold and cubed
- 3/4 cup buttermilk

For the Gravy:
- 1 pound pork sausage (usually breakfast sausage)
- 1/4 cup all-purpose flour
- 3 cups whole milk
- Salt and black pepper to taste
Optional: Red pepper flakes

Instructions

1. In a bowl, mix 2 cups flour, baking powder, baking soda, and salt.

2. Add cold, cubed butter; blend.

3. Pour in buttermilk; stir until just combined.

4. Pat dough, cut biscuits.

5. Bake at 450°F until golden. Approx 10 minutes.

6. Meanwhile, cook pork sausage in a pan.

7. Sprinkle flour over cooked sausage; stir.

8. Gradually add milk; whisk until thickened.

9. Season with salt, black pepper, and optional red pepper flakes.

10. Serve over warm biscuits.

Antebellum Era (1846-1861)

Shrimp & Grits

Shrimp and Grits, a Southern culinary icon, originated in the Lowcountry of South Carolina and Georgia. Emerging from humble beginnings as a fisherman's breakfast, the dish evolved into a savory masterpiece celebrated across the United States. In the 1980s, chefs elevated Shrimp and Grits from a regional favorite to a gourmet delicacy, adding culinary twists and variations. Combining the creamy texture of stone-ground grits with succulent shrimp, often accompanied by flavorful sauces and toppings like bacon or cheese, the dish exemplifies the fusion of Southern flavors. Today, Shrimp and Grits stands as a symbol of Southern culinary innovation and comfort. Optional: Top with crumbled bacon or andouille sausage for an extra kick. A Southern classic blending creamy grits with succulent shrimp for a flavor explosion! h hot sauce on the side.

Ingredients

For the Grits:
- 1 cup stone-ground grits
- 4 cups water or chicken broth
- Salt and black pepper to taste
- 1/2 cup shredded cheese (cheddar or Gouda), optional
- 2 tablespoons unsalted butter

For the Shrimp:
- 1 pound large shrimp, peeled and deveined
- Salt, black pepper, and paprika to season
- 2 tablespoons olive oil
- 4 cloves garlic, minced
- 1 cup cherry tomatoes, halved
- 1/4 cup chicken broth
- 2 tablespoons fresh lemon juice
- Fresh parsley for garnish

Instructions

1. Cook stone-ground grits in water or broth, season with salt and pepper. Add cheese and butter for extra richness.

2. Meanwhile, season shrimp with salt, pepper, and paprika. Sauté in olive oil with minced garlic until pink.

3. Add cherry tomatoes, chicken broth, and lemon juice; simmer until tomatoes soften.

4. Serve shrimp over creamy grits, garnish with fresh parsley.

Antebellum Era (1846-1861)

Jambalaya

Jambalaya, deeply rooted in Louisiana's culinary tapestry, is a flavorful result of multicultural influences—Spanish, French, African, and Caribbean traditions converging in this iconic dish. Adapted from the Spanish "paella," it seamlessly incorporates local ingredients like shrimp, sausage, and chicken, expertly seasoned with aromatic spices. The term "jambalaya," derived from the Provencal "jambalaia," encapsulates the dish's essence as a harmonious mix. Versatile and communal, jambalaya has become a staple, symbolizing Louisiana's cultural fusion and providing a delicious centerpiece for social gatherings and festivals. Its journey embodies the spirit of shared traditions, showcasing the region's vibrant and diverse culinary heritage.

Ingredients

- 1 lb (about 450g) smoked sausage, sliced
- 1 lb (about 450g) chicken breasts or thighs, diced
- 1 large onion, chopped
- 1 bell pepper, chopped
- 3 celery stalks, chopped
- 3 cloves garlic, minced
- 1 can (14 oz) diced tomatoes
- 1 1/2 cups long-grain rice
- 3 cups chicken broth
- 2 teaspoons Cajun seasoning
- Salt and pepper to taste
- Green onions and parsley for garnish (optional)

Instructions

1. Sauté sliced sausage until browned. Set aside.

2. Brown diced chicken. Set aside.

3. Sauté onion, bell pepper, celery, and garlic until softened.

4. Add diced tomatoes, rice, chicken broth, Cajun seasoning, salt, and pepper. Stir.

5. Bring to a boil, then simmer covered for 20-25 minutes until rice is cooked.

6. Stir in cooked sausage and chicken. Cook for 5 more minutes. Serve.

Antebellum Era (1846-1861)

Fried Green Tomatoes

Fried Green Tomatoes, a Southern culinary delight, emerged from the need to use unripe tomatoes before the frost. Originating in the American South, particularly during the Great Depression, resourceful cooks devised this dish to minimize food waste. Sliced green tomatoes are coated in cornmeal or flour, then fried to a golden crisp, creating a savory and tangy treat. The dish gained widespread popularity with the release of the novel "Fried Green Tomatoes at the Whistle Stop Cafe" and its film adaptation, turning a regional specialty into a symbol of comfort food nostalgia. Often served with a zesty dipping sauce or a side of creamy remoulade, Fried Green Tomatoes offer a delightful contrast of crunchy exterior and tender, tangy interior. The dish's popularity has extended beyond the South, becoming a beloved appetizer or accompaniment in various American restaurants. The simplicity of its preparation and the unique flavor profile continue to make Fried Green Tomatoes a timeless and versatile dish, appreciated for its historical roots and mouthwatering appeal.

Ingredients

- 4-6 green tomatoes, firm and unripe
- 1 cup buttermilk
- 1 cup cornmeal or all-purpose flour (or a mix)
- Salt and black pepper to taste
- 1/2 teaspoon cayenne pepper (optional, for added heat)
- Vegetable oil for frying

For Dipping Sauce:
- 1/2 cup mayonnaise
- 2 tablespoons Dijon mustard
- 1 tablespoon pickle relish
- 1 clove garlic, minced
- Salt and black pepper to taste

Instructions

1. Slice firm green tomatoes.

2. Dip in buttermilk.

3. Coat with a mix of cornmeal/flour, salt, pepper, and optional cayenne.

4. Fry until golden brown in vegetable oil.

5. For a tangy dip, mix mayo, Dijon mustard, pickle relish, minced garlic, salt, and pepper.

6. Serve the crispy tomatoes with the zesty sauce.

Antebellum Era (1846-1861)

Boiled Peanuts

Boiled Peanuts, a cherished Southern snack, have a history deeply rooted in the agricultural landscapes of the region. Introduced by African American farmers, this culinary tradition began as a practical way to preserve excess peanut crops. Slow-boiling green or raw peanuts in brine or seasoned water became a popular method, resulting in a unique soft texture and savory taste. Emerging during the late 19th and early 20th centuries, boiled peanuts quickly became a staple at roadside stands and gatherings, embodying the essence of Southern comfort food. Today, these briny treats remain an iconic snack, symbolizing the intersection of agriculture, culinary creativity, and Southern hospitality.

Ingredients

- 1 pound raw or green peanuts (in-shell)
- 1/2 cup salt (adjust to taste)
- 1-2 tablespoons Cajun seasoning (optional)
- 1-2 teaspoons red pepper flakes (adjust to spice preference)
- Water

Instructions

1. Rinse raw peanuts in-shell.

2. In a large pot, combine peanuts, salt, Cajun seasoning (optional), and red pepper flakes.

3. Cover with water.

4. Bring to a boil, then simmer for 4-6 hours or until peanuts reach desired tenderness.

5. Taste and adjust salt/spice.

6. Drain and serve warm.

Antebellum Era (1846-1861)

Sonker (North Carolina dessert)

Sonker, a cherished dessert originating in North Carolina's Surry County, carries a flavorful history deeply embedded in the region's culinary tapestry. Emerging in the early 20th century, Sonker has its roots in the traditional fruit cobblers of the area, with a distinctive twist that sets it apart. Commonly filled with sweet potatoes, apples, or berries, Sonker boasts a unique crust-to-filling ratio, featuring a crustless or minimally covered fruit filling. This approach allows the vibrant flavors of the fruit to shine through, creating a delightful harmony with the biscuit-like dough topping. Traditionally, Sonker has been a communal dish, baked in family kitchens and community gatherings, embodying the spirit of shared traditions and familial connections. Celebrated in local festivals like the Sonker Festival in Mount Airy, this dessert remains a cherished symbol of North Carolina's culinary heritage.

Ingredients

For the Filling:
- 4-5 cups of fruit (sweet potatoes, apples, berries), peeled and sliced
- 1 cup granulated sugar
- 1 teaspoon ground cinnamon
- 1/2 teaspoon ground nutmeg
- 1/4 teaspoon salt
- 1 tablespoon lemon juice (for berries)

For the Dough:
- 2 cups all-purpose flour
- 1/2 cup granulated sugar
- 2 teaspoons baking powder
- 1/2 teaspoon salt
- 1 cup milk
- 1/2 cup unsalted butter, melted

Instructions

1. Mix fruit with sugar, cinnamon, nutmeg, salt, and lemon juice (for berries).

2. In a separate bowl, combine flour, sugar, baking powder, salt, milk, and melted butter for the dough.

3. Spread fruit mixture in a baking dish, dollop spoonfuls of dough on top.

4. Bake at 350°F (175°C) for approximately 45-60 minutes until fruit is bubbly and the crust is golden.

5. Serve warm with whipped cream or vanilla ice cream.

Antebellum Era (1846-1861)

Red Beans & Rice

Red Beans and Rice, a beloved American dish, has deep roots tracing back to West African, Spanish, and Creole culinary influences. Introduced to the United States through the African diaspora, the dish evolved in Louisiana, particularly in New Orleans. Originally a Monday tradition—laundry day, it allowed simmering beans while occupied with chores. The addition of aromatic vegetables, spicy Andouille sausage, and Creole spices created a flavorful, one-pot wonder. Red Beans and Rice became a staple, symbolizing resilience and resourcefulness. Over time, it transcended socio-economic boundaries, uniting diverse communities through a shared appreciation for this comforting and culturally rich dish, embodying the soulful spirit of American cuisine.

Ingredients

- 1 pound dried red kidney beans, soaked overnight
- 1 pound Andouille sausage, sliced
- 1 large onion, finely chopped
- 1 bell pepper, diced
- 2 celery stalks, diced
- 4 cloves garlic, minced
- 2 bay leaves
- 1 teaspoon dried thyme
- 1 teaspoon dried oregano
- 1 teaspoon paprika
- 1/2 teaspoon cayenne pepper (adjust to taste)
- Salt and black pepper to taste
- 6 cups chicken or vegetable broth
- 2 cups long-grain white rice
- Green onions and parsley for garnish

Instructions

1. Soak kidney beans overnight.

2. Sauté Andouille sausage, onion, bell pepper, celery, and garlic until veggies are soft.

3. Add drained beans, bay leaves, thyme, oregano, paprika, cayenne, salt, pepper, and broth.

4. Simmer until beans are tender.

5. Meanwhile, cook rice separately.

6. Mash some beans for thickness.

7. Serve beans over rice, garnish with green onions and parsley.

Antebellum Era (1846-1861)

Baltimore Peach Cake

Baltimore Peach Cake, a delectable American treat, has a history intertwined with the vibrant culinary landscape of Maryland. Originating in the 19th century, this dessert pays homage to the region's abundant peach orchards and German baking traditions. The cake features a yeast-based dough, generously topped with fresh, sliced peaches, and often sprinkled with a crumbly streusel. Over time, Baltimore Peach Cake became a cherished part of local celebrations, picnics, and family gatherings, embodying the spirit of community and the bountiful summer harvest. Its enduring popularity showcases the delightful fusion of German culinary heritage with the agricultural richness of Maryland, offering a sweet taste of tradition in every slice.

Ingredients

- 1 packet active dry yeast
- 1 cup warm milk
- 1/2 cup granulated sugar
- 1/4 cup unsalted butter, melted
- 3 cups all-purpose flour
- 1/2 teaspoon salt
- 4-5 ripe peaches, sliced
- 1/4 cup brown sugar
- 1 teaspoon ground cinnamon

Instructions

1. Dissolve yeast in warm milk, add sugar, melted butter, flour, and salt.

2. Knead until smooth, let it rise.

3. Roll out dough, place in a greased pan, and let it rise again.

4. Arrange sliced peaches on the dough, sprinkle with a mix of brown sugar and cinnamon.

5. Bake at 350°F until golden- approx 25 minutes.

Antebellum Era (1846-1861)

Pickled Watermelon Rind

Pickled Watermelon Rind, a Southern culinary gem, emerged from resourcefulness and a commitment to minimizing food waste. Originating during times when frugality was crucial, particularly in the South, this practice involved preserving the often-discarded watermelon rind. By utilizing a simple brine of vinegar, sugar, and spices, cooks transformed the rind into a tangy, sweet-and-sour delicacy. Commonly seasoned with cloves, cinnamon, and ginger, the pickling process enhanced the rind's texture and flavor. Pickled Watermelon Rind gained popularity as a refreshing and sustainable treat, enjoyed during hot Southern summers and appearing at family gatherings and picnics. This practice of transforming a part of the watermelon that would have been discarded into a flavorful and unique delicacy reflects the ingenuity and culinary traditions deeply rooted in Southern culture. Today, Pickled Watermelon Rind remains a delightful testament to the region's history of thriftiness and gastronomic creativity.

Ingredients

- 4-6 cups watermelon rind, peeled and cut into bite-sized pieces
- 2 cups white vinegar
- 2 cups water
- 2 cups granulated sugar
- 1 tablespoon salt
- 1 tablespoon whole cloves
- 2 cinnamon sticks
- 1 tablespoon fresh ginger, sliced

Optional: Red pepper flakes for a hint of heat

Instructions

1. Peel and chop watermelon rind into bite-sized pieces.

2. In a pot, combine water, vinegar, sugar, salt, cloves, cinnamon, and ginger.

3. Bring to a boil, then simmer until sugar dissolves.

4. Cool slightly.

5. Pour over watermelon rind in a jar.

6. Let it cool completely, then refrigerate for 24 hours.

7. Optional: Add red pepper flakes for a kick.

Antebellum Era (1846-1861)

Chicken & Dumplings

Chicken and Dumplings, an American classic, encapsulates a history of resourcefulness, comfort, and regional culinary diversity. Rooted in European traditions, early settlers adapted their recipes to utilize locally available ingredients. This dish reached new heights during the Great Depression when cost-effective, hearty meals were essential. Variations emerged across the United States, with Southern versions favoring a rolled, flat dumpling, while the Midwest leaned towards drop dumplings. The quintessential pairing of slow-cooked chicken, aromatic broth, and tender dumplings became a symbol of warmth and sustenance, offering solace during challenging times. Today, Chicken and Dumplings stands as a testament to the evolution of American cuisine, reflecting a blend of immigrant influences and a commitment to transforming humble ingredients into a beloved, timeless comfort dish.

Ingredients

For the Chicken Stew:
- 1 whole chicken, cut into pieces (or bone-in chicken parts)
- 1 onion, chopped
- 2 carrots, sliced
- 2 celery stalks, sliced
- 3 cloves garlic, minced
- 1 bay leaf
- Salt and black pepper to taste
- 6 cups chicken broth
- 1/2 cup unsalted butter
- 1 cup all-purpose flour (for thickening)

For the Dumplings:
- 2 cups all-purpose flour
- 1 tablespoon baking powder
- 1/2 teaspoon salt

- 1 cup milk
- 1/4 cup unsalted butter, melted

Instructions

1. Simmer whole chicken with veggies, bay leaf, salt, and pepper in broth until tender.

2. Remove and shred chicken.

3. Make a roux with butter and flour until golden.

4. Gradually add broth for a thickened stew and Season with salt and pepper.

6. Return shredded chicken to the pot.

7. For dumplings, mix flour, baking powder, salt, milk, and melted butter.

8. Drop spoonfuls into the simmering stew. Cover and cook until dumplings are done.

10. Serve hot, garnished with fresh parsley.

Civil War Era (1861-1865)

(Updated) Hardtack

Hardtack, a durable and simple sustenance, holds a storied history as a staple ration in the diets of sailors, soldiers, and explorers throughout centuries. Dating back to ancient civilizations, its popularity soared during the Age of Sail and the American Civil War. Comprising only flour, water, and salt, hardtack provided sustenance for long journeys, as it was resistant to spoilage. Its dense, dry nature earned it the moniker "tooth dullers" or "molar breakers." This inexpensive, non-perishable biscuit symbolized endurance and survival. Though basic, hardtack played a crucial role in sustaining troops during arduous campaigns, showcasing its enduring significance in military and maritime history as a symbol of resilience and a testament to the resourcefulness of those who relied on it. Below is the updated, modernized recipe for a cook that wants to taste history without having to sacrifice flavour or taste.

Ingredients

- 3 cups all-purpose flour
- 1 cup whole wheat flour (for a nuttier flavor)
- 1 teaspoon baking powder
- 1 teaspoon salt
- 1/4 cup honey or maple syrup (for sweetness)
- 1 cup water (adjust as needed)

Instructions

1. Mix 3 cups all-purpose and 1 cup whole wheat flour, 1 tsp baking powder, and a pinch of salt.

2. Add 1/4 cup honey or maple syrup, slowly blend in water for a stiff dough.

3. Roll, cut, and prick.

4. Bake at 375°F for 15-20 mins.

Variation
Savoury Hardtack

Add 1/2 cup grated Parmesan or sharp cheddar cheese and 1 teaspoon cracked black pepper to the dough before baking for a savory hardtack.

Civil War Era (1861-1865)

Molasses Cookies

Molasses Cookies, with their rich, spiced flavor and chewy texture, have a history deeply embedded in American culinary heritage. Rooted in the nation's early days, when molasses was a common sweetener, these cookies evolved from traditional British gingerbreads. As the American colonies embraced molasses imported from the Caribbean, it became a staple in kitchens. The addition of spices like cinnamon, ginger, and cloves transformed these treats into a uniquely American delight. Molasses Cookies gained prominence during the 19th century, and recipes were passed down through generations. Their popularity soared during wartime when rationing encouraged creative use of available ingredients. Today, Molasses Cookies stand as a nostalgic reminder of the past, embodying the sweet, spiced essence of American history in every delicious bite.

Ingredients

- 2 1/4 cups all-purpose flour
- 1 teaspoon baking soda
- 1/2 teaspoon salt
- 1 teaspoon ground ginger
- 1 teaspoon ground cinnamon
- 1/2 teaspoon ground cloves
- 3/4 cup unsalted butter, softened
- 1 cup granulated sugar
- 1 large egg
- 1/4 cup molasses
- 1 teaspoon vanilla extract
- Granulated sugar (for rolling, optional)

Optional Additions:
- 1/2 cup chopped crystallized ginger for extra zing
- Powdered sugar for dusting after baking

Instructions

1. In a bowl, mix 2 1/4 cups flour, 1 tsp baking soda, 1/2 tsp salt, 1 tsp each of ginger, cinnamon, and 1/2 tsp cloves.

2. Cream 3/4 cup softened butter with 1 cup sugar.

3. Add 1 egg, 1/4 cup molasses, and 1 tsp vanilla.

4. Gradually add dry ingredients.

5. Optional: Stir in chopped crystallized ginger.

6. Roll into balls, coat with sugar if desired.

7. Bake at 350°F for 10-12 mins.

8. Dust with powdered sugar if you like.

Civil War Era (1861-1865)

Bean Soup

Civil War Bean Soup, a testament to resourcefulness during a tumultuous era, traces its origins to the American Civil War. Soldiers faced scarcity and relied on basic, shelf-stable ingredients like dried beans to sustain themselves. The simplicity of this soup made it a practical and hearty meal for troops in challenging conditions. Reflecting the ingenuity of the time, this dish thrived on minimal resources, showcasing the resilient spirit of those who prepared and consumed it. Over the years, the recipe evolved, incorporating diverse ingredients while preserving its historical roots. Today, Civil War Bean Soup stands as a culinary homage to the past, offering a taste of the fortitude and creativity that sustained individuals during a pivotal period in American history. This enduring dish continues to symbolize both the struggle for survival and the adaptability that defines the nation's culinary heritage.

Ingredients

- 1 pound dried navy beans, soaked overnight
- 1 ham hock or smoked ham bone
- 1 onion, finely chopped
- 2 carrots, diced
- 2 celery stalks, diced
- 3 cloves garlic, minced
- 1 bay leaf
- Salt and black pepper to taste
- 6 cups chicken or vegetable broth
- 2 tablespoons vegetable oil

Optional Additions:
- 1 teaspoon dried thyme
- 1 teaspoon dried rosemary
- 1 cup diced tomatoes

Instructions

1. Sauté onions, carrots, celery, and garlic.

2. Add soaked beans, ham hock, bay leaf, and herbs.

3. Pour in broth, simmer for 1.5-2 hours until beans are tender.

4. Remove ham hock, shred meat, return to pot.

5. Season with salt, pepper, and optional tomatoes.

Variation
Sweet Potato Surprise:

Incorporate diced sweet potatoes along with the carrots for a touch of sweetness and a vibrant color contrast. They will add a unique twist to the classic recipe.

Civil War Era (1861-1865)

Molasses Taffy

Molasses Taffy, a cherished sweet treat with roots tracing back to the Civil War era, epitomizes a confectionery tradition born out of necessity and creativity. During this tumultuous period, traditional sugar supplies were scarce, leading to the adaptation of molasses—a more readily available sweetener. In the simplicity of home kitchens, families combined molasses with sugar and butter, boiling the mixture until it reached a chewy taffy consistency. This humble candy not only provided a delightful respite from wartime hardships but also showcased the ingenuity of homemakers in making do with available resources. Molasses Taffy became a symbol of resilience and sweetness in the face of adversity, transcending its humble origins to become a cherished part of American culinary history that continues to evoke the flavors and spirit of a bygone era.

Ingredients

- 1 cup molasses
- 1 cup granulated sugar
- 1/4 cup unsalted butter
- 1/2 teaspoon vanilla extract
- 1/4 teaspoon baking soda

Optional for Flavor Variation:
- Sea salt for a salted molasses taffy
- Chopped nuts for added texture
- Grated orange or lemon zest for citrus-infused taffy

Instructions

1. In a pot, combine 1 cup molasses, 1 cup sugar, and 1/4 cup butter.

2. Boil until it reaches a taffy consistency—use a candy thermometer if available.

3. Stir in 1/2 tsp vanilla extract and 1/4 tsp baking soda.

4. Optional: Add sea salt, nuts, or citrus zest for extra flavor.

5. Pour onto a buttered surface to cool.

6. Once cool enough to handle, pull until it turns glossy and light in color.

7. Twist into individual pieces.

Civil War Era (1861-1865)

Confederate Hash

Confederate Hash, a resilient dish born during the Civil War, reflects the resourceful and inventive spirit of Southern cooking amidst adversity. As Union blockades limited food supplies, Southerners crafted meals from meager ingredients. Confederate Hash emerged as a flavorful concoction blending leftover meats, typically salted pork or corned beef, with potatoes, onions, and spices. Cooked together in a skillet until crispy and golden, this hash provided sustenance during challenging times. Its adaptability allowed families to make the most of available provisions, turning leftovers into a hearty and satisfying meal. Confederate Hash not only served as a practical solution to wartime shortages but also became a symbol of Southern culinary ingenuity, embodying the resilience and creativity of a region determined to nourish itself despite the constraints imposed by conflict.

Ingredients

- 2 cups leftover cooked meat (salted pork, corned beef, or any cooked meat of choice), diced
- 2 cups potatoes, peeled and diced
- 1 cup onion, finely chopped
- Salt and black pepper to taste
- Butter or oil for frying

Optional Additions:
- Bell peppers, diced
- Worcestershire sauce for extra flavor
- Fresh herbs like thyme or rosemary

Instructions

1. In a skillet, cook 2 cups diced leftover meat, 2 cups diced potatoes, and 1 cup chopped onions in butter or oil.

2. Season with salt and pepper.

3. Optional: Add diced bell peppers and a dash of Worcestershire sauce for extra flavor.

4. Cook until crispy and golden.

Variation
Mushroom and Swiss Upgrade:

Incorporate sautéed mushrooms into the hash mix. Melt Swiss cheese on top during the final minutes of cooking for a creamy and earthy delight.

Civil War Era (1861-1865)

Tomato & Peach Corn Dodgers

Corn Dodgers, a humble and staple dish during the Civil War era, encapsulate the resourcefulness of Southern cooking amid scarcity. As the conflict disrupted supply chains, Southerners turned to readily available ingredients like cornmeal to sustain themselves. Corn Dodgers, a precursor to modern cornbread, were simple mixtures of cornmeal, water, and salt, shaped into small, oblong cakes, and cooked on hot surfaces or open flames. These frugal yet nourishing morsels became a dietary staple for soldiers and civilians alike. Their dense texture and portable nature made them convenient for soldiers on the move. Corn Dodgers symbolize the ingenuity of Southern homemakers who, faced with limited resources, transformed basic ingredients into a sustaining and culturally significant dish, leaving an indelible mark on the culinary legacy of the American South. We are going with some modern additions to make this one stand out!

Ingredients

- 1 cup cornmeal
- 1 cup all-purpose flour
- 1 tablespoon sugar
- 1 teaspoon baking powder
- 1/2 teaspoon baking soda
- 1/2 teaspoon salt
- 1/2 cup unsalted butter, cold and cubed
- 1/2 cup buttermilk
- 1 large egg
- 1/2 cup fresh corn kernels
- 1/2 cup ripe tomatoes, finely diced
- 1/2 cup ripe peaches, finely diced
- 2 tablespoons chopped fresh herbs (such as chives, thyme, and parsley)

Instructions

1. Mix: 1 cup cornmeal, 1 cup flour, 1 tbsp sugar, 1 tsp baking powder, 1/2 tsp baking soda, 1/2 tsp salt.

2. Add: 1/2 cup each of diced tomatoes, diced peaches, fresh corn, & 2 tbsp herbs.

3. Bake at 375°F for 15-18 mins.

4. Serve with Herb-Infused Cream Cheese Dip, Guacamole, or Salsa Fresca.

Civil War Era (1861-1865)

Boiled Salted Meat

During the Civil War, boiled salted meat emerged as a staple for soldiers due to its practicality and longevity. This straightforward yet essential dish involved simmering salted meat, often pork or beef, in water until tender. The salt not only preserved the meat but also added flavor, a critical factor when dealing with limited resources. Soldiers relied on this sustenance during long campaigns, as it provided a reliable source of protein and essential nutrients. Boiled salted meat could be easily prepared in camp kitchens, offering a hot and filling meal for troops facing the harsh realities of war. Despite its simplicity, this dish played a crucial role in sustaining soldiers and became emblematic of the challenges faced on both sides of the conflict, highlighting the resourcefulness required during this tumultuous period in American history.

Ingredients

- 3-4 pounds of fresh pork or beef (cuts like pork belly, shoulder, or beef brisket work well)
- 1 cup kosher salt (or coarse sea salt)
- 1/2 cup brown sugar
- 2 tablespoons black peppercorns, crushed
- 2 bay leaves, crushed
- 4 cloves garlic, minced (optional)

Instructions

1. Select 3-4 lbs of fresh pork or beef, trim, and rinse thoroughly.

2. Create a flavor-packed cure with 1 cup kosher salt, 1/2 cup brown sugar, crushed peppercorns, bay leaves, and minced garlic.

3. Massage the mixture onto the meat, ensuring full coverage, and seal it in a bag or container.

4. Refrigerate for 3-5 days, turning occasionally for an even cure.

5. Rinse off excess salt; if desired, soak to taste preference.

6. Pat dry and air-dry in the fridge for 1-2 days to develop a pellicle.

7. Reheat with vegetable or use in a sandwich.

Variation
Coffee and Cocoa Rub:

Create a dry rub with finely ground coffee beans and cocoa powder. Apply this rub to the cured meat before air-drying to impart deep, rich flavors.

Civil War Era (1861-1865)

Union Pudding

Union Pudding, a delightful dessert from the Civil War era, reflects a time when resourcefulness was key in creating satisfying meals. Comprising simple ingredients, this comforting dish unites flour, suet, molasses, and spices, showcasing the ingenuity of home cooks during challenging times. The suet, or beef fat, provides richness and moisture to the pudding, while molasses imparts a deep, robust sweetness. A blend of spices, often cinnamon and nutmeg, adds warmth and complexity. The pudding is traditionally steamed or boiled, resulting in a dense and moist texture. Union Pudding embodies the spirit of making the most of available ingredients, offering a taste of history that transcends its humble components. As a symbol of unity, it resonates with a time when communities faced adversity together, finding solace and sweetness in a simple yet enduring treat.

Ingredients

- 1 cup suet (beef fat), finely chopped
- 1 cup molasses
- 1 cup milk
- 2 cups all-purpose flour
- 1 teaspoon baking soda
- 1 teaspoon ground cinnamon
- 1/2 teaspoon ground nutmeg
- A pinch of salt

Instructions

1. Mix 1 cup finely chopped suet, 1 cup molasses, and 1 cup milk.

2. In another bowl, combine 2 cups flour, 1 tsp baking soda, 1 tsp cinnamon, 1/2 tsp nutmeg, and a pinch of salt.

3. Gradually blend the wet and dry ingredients, then pour into a greased pudding mold.

4. Bake at 350°F for 1.5-2 hours in a water bath until firm.

Variation
Spiced Apple Compote'

Stir 1-1.5 cups diced apples with cinnamon, nutmeg. Swirl compote into pudding batter before baking for fruity bursts.

Civil War Era (1861-1865)

Salted Cajun Fish Jerky

During the Civil War era, salted fish and various forms of jerky were common components of soldiers' rations. While historical records don't explicitly use the term "Salted Fish Jerky," fish preservation methods involved salting and drying, creating a type of fish jerky. Soldiers relied on these preserved foods due to their practicality, ease of transportation, and extended shelf life. The term "Salted Fish Jerky" may not be explicitly documented, but the historical context supports the use of salted and dried fish as part of the soldiers' diets during the war. The specific types of jerky and preserved foods varied based on the region, available resources, and logistical considerations. Overall, these preservation techniques played a crucial role in providing a reliable source of sustenance for troops during a challenging period in American history.

Ingredients

- 1 pound fresh fish fillets (such as catfish or trout), sliced into thin strips
- 2 tablespoons sea salt
- 1 tablespoon cayenne pepper
- 1 tablespoon paprika
- 1 teaspoon onion powder
- 1 teaspoon garlic powder

Instructions

1. Slice 1 lb of fresh fish (catfish or trout) into thin strips.

2. Mix 2 tbsp sea salt, 1 tbsp cayenne pepper, 1 tbsp paprika, 1 tsp onion powder, and 1 tsp garlic powder.

3. Coat fish strips with the spice mixture and let sit in the refrigerator for 2-3 hours before dehydrating

4. Oven-dry fish jerky at 150°F for 4-6 hours. Arrange on racks, prop oven door open, and check for firm, leathery texture. Cool before storing. Or, use a dehydrator and follow manufacturer's directions, until jerky consistency is reached.

Reconstruction Era (1865-1877)

Tomato Marmalade

Tomato Marmalade, a delectable preserve of the Reconstruction Era, epitomizes the ingenuity of resourceful cooks during a time of post-Civil War rebuilding. Amidst limited resources, the humble tomato, often regarded as an ornamental fruit, was transformed into a sweet and tangy delicacy. Simmered with sugar, spices, and sometimes vinegar, tomatoes underwent a flavorful metamorphosis into a luscious marmalade, capturing the essence of a fruitful harvest. This culinary innovation not only provided a burst of taste to meager meals but also showcased the resilience and adaptability of Southern kitchens. Spread on biscuits or served alongside savory dishes, Tomato Marmalade reflected the era's commitment to making the most of available ingredients, leaving a delicious legacy that echoes the spirit of Reconstruction.

Ingredients

- 8 cups ripe tomatoes, peeled, seeded, and chopped
- 4 cups granulated sugar
- 1 lemon, juiced and zested
- 1 orange, juiced and zested
- 1 cinnamon stick
- 1 teaspoon whole cloves
- 1/2 teaspoon ground ginger
- Pinch of salt

Instructions

1. Chop 8 cups of ripe tomatoes.

2. Add 4 cups sugar, lemon, and orange zest and juice.

3. Toss in a spice bundle with cinnamon, cloves, and ginger.

4. Simmer for 1-2 hours until jammy.

5. Test on a plate for wrinkles, remove spices, and jar.

6. Spread on toast or pair with savory dishes for a trip to the past.

Reconstruction Era (1865-1877)

Mushroom Gravy Grits

During the Reconstruction Era, the South experienced profound social and economic changes, and the culinary landscape adapted accordingly. The vegetarian Mushroom Gravy Grits of this era reflect a shift in dietary habits and resourcefulness. With the scarcity of meat and the need for economical yet flavorful meals, cooks turned to locally available ingredients. Mushrooms, abundant and flavorful, became a staple in Southern kitchens, offering a meaty alternative. The preparation of mushroom gravy, rich with herbs and spices, became a symbol of inventive and wholesome cooking. Paired with creamy stone-ground grits, this dish not only embodied the era's culinary adaptability but also echoed a growing consciousness about sustainable and vegetarian choices. The Vegetarian Mushroom Gravy Grits of the Reconstruction Era represent a chapter in Southern cuisine where resilience and creativity converged to bring forth a delicious and comforting dish that spoke to the changing times.

Ingredients

For the Mushroom Gravy:
- 2 cups assorted fresh mushrooms (such as cremini, shiitake, or button), sliced
- 2 tablespoons unsalted butter
- 2 tablespoons all-purpose flour
- 2 cups vegetable broth
- 1 teaspoon soy sauce
- 1 teaspoon Worcestershire sauce (ensure it's vegetarian)
- 1/2 teaspoon dried thyme
- Salt and black pepper to taste

For the Grits:
- 1 cup stone-ground grits
- 4 cups water
- 1 cup milk (optional for creamier grits)

Instructions

1. Sauté assorted mushrooms in 2 tablespoons of butter until golden.
2. Introduce 2 tablespoons of flour, stirring to form a roux.
3. Gradually incorporate 2 cups of vegetable broth, 1 teaspoon each of soy sauce and Worcestershire sauce, 1/2 teaspoon of dried thyme, and salt and pepper to taste.
4. Simmer until the mixture reaches the desired thickness, adjusting seasoning accordingly.
5. In a separate pot, bring 4 cups of water (or a combination of water and 1 cup of milk) to a boil.
6. Whisk in 1 cup of stone-ground grits, simmering until thickened.
7. Season the grits with salt and serve in bowls, generously topped with the prepared vegetarian mushroom gravy.
8. Optionally, garnish with chopped fresh parsley or chives for added freshness.

Reconstruction Era (1865-1877)

Braised Pork Belly

Braised Pork Belly, a testament to the culinary ingenuity of the Reconstruction Era, emerged as a flavorsome and resourceful dish during a period of post-Civil War rebuilding. In an era marked by scarcity and economic challenges, pork belly, an affordable and versatile cut, became a staple. Braised slowly in a medley of aromatic herbs, spices, and often accompanied by locally grown vegetables, this dish exemplified the resilience and resourcefulness of Southern kitchens. The slow-cooking method not only tenderized the pork belly but also allowed flavors to meld, creating a rich and comforting meal. Served on dining tables and in humble kitchens alike, Braised Pork Belly embodied the spirit of adapting to the times, transforming simple ingredients into a dish that carried the legacy of Reconstruction-era culinary traditions.

Ingredients

For the Pork Belly:
- 2 pounds pork belly, skin on
- Salt and black pepper to season

For the Braising Liquid:
- 2 cups chicken or beef broth
- 1 cup dry red wine
- 1/4 cup soy sauce
- 1/4 cup apple cider vinegar
- 2 tablespoons brown sugar
- 1 onion, thinly sliced
- 4 cloves garlic, minced
- 2 bay leaves
- 1 teaspoon dried thyme
- 1 teaspoon dried rosemary
- 1 teaspoon smoked paprika
- 1/2 teaspoon ground cumin

Instructions

1. Preheat your oven to 325°F.

2. Score the pork belly skin, season, and brown until golden.

3. In a bowl, mix 2 cups broth, 1 cup red wine, 1/4 cup soy sauce, 1/4 cup apple cider vinegar, 2 tbsp brown sugar, sliced onion, garlic, bay leaves, thyme, rosemary, smoked paprika, and cumin.

4. Place the pork in a Dutch oven, pour the braising liquid, and bake for 2.5-3 hours.

5. For the last 30 minutes, uncover and crisp the skin at 400°F.

6. Rest before slicing, drizzle with reduced liquid, and garnish with parsley if desired.

Reconstruction Era (1865-1877)

Chess Pie

Chess Pie, a classic dessert hailing from the Reconstruction Era, encapsulates the essence of simplicity and indulgence amid post-Civil War challenges. With basic pantry staples like butter, sugar, eggs, and a touch of vinegar or buttermilk, this pie exemplified resourcefulness in Southern kitchens. The origin of the name is shrouded in mystery, with various tales suggesting "just pie" or "chest pie," reflecting its uncomplicated nature. In a period marked by economic hardships, Chess Pie's straightforward yet delectable ingredients provided a sweet respite. Whether enjoyed on a rustic farmhouse table or a city parlour, this custard-like pie, with its crisp crust and sweet filling, embodied the spirit of making do with what was readily available. A slice of Chess Pie from the Reconstruction Era not only offered a momentary escape from adversity but also became a timeless symbol of comfort and culinary ingenuity.

Ingredients

For the Filling:
- 1 1/2 cups granulated sugar
- 1 tablespoon cornmeal
- 1 tablespoon all-purpose flour
- 1/4 teaspoon salt
- 1/2 cup unsalted butter, melted
- 1/4 cup whole milk
- 1 teaspoon white vinegar
- 1 teaspoon vanilla extract
- 4 large eggs

plus:
- 1 pre-made 9-inch pie crust

Instructions

1. Using a pre-made 9-inch pie crust, whisk together 1.5 cups sugar, 1 tbsp each of cornmeal and flour, 1/4 tsp salt, 1/2 cup melted butter, 1/4 cup milk, 1 tsp white vinegar, 1 tsp vanilla extract, and 4 eggs.

2. Pour the silky filling into the crust.

3. Bake at 350°F for 45-50 minutes until set.

4. Cool and slice for a taste of timeless Southern sweetness.

Reconstruction Era (1865-1877)

Quick Pickled Okra

Pickled Okra, a staple of Southern cuisine with roots extending to the Reconstruction Era, is a culinary gem that embodies the art of preserving seasonal harvests. This tangy delicacy is a testament to resourcefulness, as farmers sought ways to extend the life of their abundant okra yields. Okra pods, known for their natural thickness, absorb a briny bath of vinegar, spices, and garlic, creating a crisp texture and a delightful medley of flavors. The pickling process not only imparts a zesty kick but also enhances the okra's innate earthiness. Often found in Mason jars on pantry shelves, Pickled Okra became a versatile companion to meals, offering a pop of acidity and crunch. Whether enjoyed solo as a snack, added to relishes, or served alongside hearty dishes, Pickled Okra stands as a testament to Southern ingenuity and the timeless allure of pickling traditions.

Ingredients

- 1 pound fresh okra
- 2 cloves garlic, peeled and crushed
- 1 teaspoon whole mustard seeds
- 1 teaspoon whole coriander seeds
- 1 teaspoon whole black peppercorns
- 1-2 dried red chili peppers (optional for heat)
- 2 cups white vinegar
- 2 cups water
- 2 tablespoons kosher salt
- 1 tablespoon sugar

Instructions

1. Wash and trim 1 pound of okra, placing them in sterilized jars.

2. Add 2 crushed garlic cloves, 1 teaspoon each of mustard seeds, coriander seeds, and black peppercorns.

3. Include 1-2 dried red chili peppers for heat.

4. In a saucepan, boil 2 cups white vinegar, 2 cups water, 2 tablespoons kosher salt, and 1 tablespoon sugar.

5. Pour the hot brine over the okra, ensuring they're fully submerged.

6. Cool, seal the jars, and refrigerate for at least 24 hours.

Reconstruction Era (1865-1877)

English Oxtail Consommé

Oxtail soup, with a rich history preceding its embrace in the U.S. during the Reconstruction Era, holds deep roots in European and Asian culinary traditions. In Europe, the utilization of oxtails in soups can be traced back to times when thriftiness and resourcefulness were paramount in the kitchen. This robust dish emerged as a testament to transforming a tough, bony cut into a flavorful delicacy, embodying the culinary ingenuity of European households. Simultaneously, across Asia, oxtail soup became a staple, celebrated for its umami-laden broth and tender meat. The dish transcended borders, embodying a harmonious blend of flavors and techniques. By the time oxtail soup found its way to the U.S. during the Reconstruction period, it carried with it a legacy of adaptability and nourishment, weaving together a global tapestry of culinary traditions. English Oxtail Consommé, our version, draws inspiration from European culinary traditions. This clear and refined consommé highlights the elegance of oxtails. Clarified and seasoned delicately, it mirrors the sophisticated tastes of the era's upper-class dining.

Ingredients

- 2 pounds oxtails, trimmed
- 2 tablespoons vegetable oil
- 1 large onion, coarsely chopped
- 2 carrots, peeled and coarsely chopped
- 2 celery stalks, coarsely chopped
- 3 cloves garlic, crushed
- 2 tomatoes, coarsely chopped
- 2 egg whites
- 4 cups beef broth
- 1 bay leaf
- 1 teaspoon whole peppercorns
- Salt to taste
- Fresh parsley for garnish

Instructions

1. Begin by searing oxtails.

2. Sauté a medley of onions, carrots, celery, garlic, and tomatoes.

3. Simmer 3-4 hours the mix with broth, bay leaf, and peppercorns.

4. Whisk frothy egg whites into the broth for clarification.

5. Strain the concoction.

6. Garnish it with fresh parsley.

7. Relish the nuanced taste of English-inspired Oxtail Consommé.

Reconstruction Era (1865-1877)

Corn & Tomato Salad

The Colonial Corn and Tomato Salad echoes the culinary landscape of the Restoration era in the United States, drawing inspiration from early American cooking traditions. During this time, fresh and locally sourced ingredients played a pivotal role in shaping colonial cuisine. Corn, a staple of the Native American diet, became intertwined with European culinary practices, evolving into a symbol of sustenance and adaptability.

This salad captures the essence of early American kitchens, combining the simplicity of corn kernels with the burst of flavor from cherry tomatoes. The addition of chives, buttermilk, and mayonnaise reflects the resourceful and straightforward approach to ingredients available during the Restoration era. By embracing Colonial influences, this salad offers a glimpse into the historical roots of American cooking, celebrating the resilience and ingenuity that shaped the nation's culinary heritage. Enjoy a taste of history with this Colonial-inspired Corn and Tomato Salad.

Ingredients

- 2 cups fresh corn kernels
- 1 cup cherry tomatoes, halved
- 2 tablespoons chives, finely chopped
- 1/4 cup buttermilk
- 2 tablespoons mayonnaise
- Salt and pepper to taste

Optional Additions:
- Crispy bacon bits for extra flavor
- Diced cucumber for freshness

Instructions

1. Toss fresh corn and halved cherry tomatoes with chopped chives.

2. Whisk buttermilk, mayo, salt, and pepper for a creamy dressing.

3. Coat the salad with the dressing, chill.

4. Optionally, add bacon or cucumber.

Reconstruction Era (1865-1877)

Bourbon Balls

Bourbon Balls, a delectable Southern delicacy with roots in the Restoration era, encapsulate the rich flavors of tradition and celebration. These bite-sized treats boast a unique blend of finely chopped pecans, powdered sugar, and vanilla wafer crumbs, bound together by the spirited essence of Kentucky bourbon. Rolled in confectioners' sugar, these indulgent balls develop a delightful boozy kick over time, making them a perfect addition to festive occasions. Originating from the South, where bourbon is deeply woven into culinary heritage, Bourbon Balls have become synonymous with hospitality and warmth. Whether served at gatherings or as homemade gifts, these little confections offer a taste of history and a nod to the enduring charm of Southern sweets. Enjoyed responsibly, Bourbon Balls are a timeless and flavorful delight that pays homage to the flavors of the past.

Ingredients

- 1 cup finely chopped pecans
- 1 cup vanilla wafer crumbs
- 1 cup powdered sugar, divided
- 2 tablespoons cocoa powder
- 2 tablespoons light corn syrup
- 1/4 cup bourbon
- Confectioners' sugar for rolling

Instructions

1. Mix 1 cup pecans, vanilla wafer crumbs, 1/2 cup powdered sugar, and cocoa.

2. Add 2 tbsp corn syrup and 1/4 cup bourbon.

3. Shape into balls and roll in powdered sugar.

4. Chill for 2 hours.

5. Optionally, roll in more sugar.

Reconstruction Era (1865-1877)

Graham Crackers

Invented by Sylvester Graham in the 1830s, Graham Crackers originated during the early 19th century, reflecting Graham's advocacy for whole grains and natural living. While the crackers were initially unsweetened and adhered to Graham's dietary principles, their popularity soared during the Restoration Era (1865-1877). The post-Civil War period witnessed increased accessibility and distribution of food products, contributing to Graham Crackers becoming a staple in households across the United States. As dietary trends evolved and convenience gained importance, these crackers found favor for their wholesome image and versatility. By the end of the 19th century, Graham Crackers had firmly entrenched themselves in American culinary culture, marking a shift towards processed snacks that would persist into the 20th century. Their journey from a niche health food to a mainstream delight mirrored the changing tastes and preferences of the Restoration Era.

Ingredients

- 2 1/2 cups whole wheat flour
- 1 teaspoon baking soda
- 1/2 teaspoon salt
- 1/2 cup unsalted butter, softened
- 1/3 cup brown sugar
- 1/4 cup honey
- 1 teaspoon vanilla extract
- 1/4 cup milk

Instructions

1. Whisk 2.5 cups whole wheat flour, 1 tsp baking soda, and 0.5 tsp salt.

2. Cream 0.5 cup softened butter, 1/3 cup brown sugar, 0.25 cup honey, and 1 tsp vanilla.

3. Gradually add the dry mix and 0.25 cup milk.

4. Chill the dough.

5. Roll out, cut shapes, and bake at 350°F for 12-15 mins.

Reconstruction Era (1865-1877)

Slow-Roasted Pork Shoulder, Collard Greens & Pimento Cheese Sandwich

During the Reconstruction Era, collard greens, pimento cheese, and slow-roasted pork played pivotal roles in shaping Southern cuisine. Collard greens, with roots in African and European traditions, thrived as a hardy, nutritious staple. Cultivated in home gardens, they were often paired with smoked meats. Pimento cheese, emerging in the early 20th century, featured diced pimentos, a commercial introduction from the late 19th century. This rich spread became a Southern favorite. Slow-roasted pork, a method born out of necessity, utilized tougher cuts cooked slowly for tenderness. Together, these culinary elements reflected the resilience and resourcefulness of the Reconstruction Era, blending diverse cultural influences to create a distinct Southern flavor profile. The combination of collards, pimento cheese, and slow-roasted pork encapsulated the era's agricultural landscape and the evolving tapestry of Southern culinary traditions.

Ingredients

- 1 pound collard greens, cleaned and chopped
- 1/2 pound slow-roasted pork shoulder, diced
- 1 tablespoon olive oil
- 1 onion, finely chopped
- 2 cloves garlic, minced
- Salt and black pepper to taste
- Cornbread slices
- Pimento cheese for topping

For Pimento Cheese:
1. Combine sharp cheddar, mayonnaise, diced pimentos, a pinch of cayenne, and garlic powder.

2. Blend until a creamy consistency is achieved.

3. Chill the mixture to allow flavors to meld.

Instructions

1. Season pork shoulder with herbs and spices.

2. Roast at 275°F for 6-8 hrs or until internal temp reaches 190°F.

3. Rest before shredding.

4. Sauté collard greens with onion and garlic.

5. Reheat shredded slow-roasted pork.

6. Spread pimento cheese on bread.

7. Layer warm pork and collards.

8. Create a sandwich, press for a melty finish.

Gilded Age (1877-1900)

Oysters Rockefeller

Oysters Rockefeller, an iconic dish, originated in the late 19th century at Antoine's restaurant in New Orleans. Created by Jules Alciatore, son of the restaurant's founder, the dish was named for the richness of its flavor, reminiscent of the Rockefeller family's wealth. The original recipe remains a closely guarded secret. However, it is known to involve a blend of finely chopped green vegetables, herbs, and a rich sauce, which is generously spooned over fresh oysters before baking. The dish gained popularity for its decadent combination of flavors and textures. Oysters Rockefeller symbolizes the opulence of the Gilded Age and has become a classic representation of New Orleans' culinary heritage, celebrated for its indulgent blend of fresh seafood and rich, flavorful ingredients.

Ingredients

- 24 fresh oysters, shucked on the half shell
- 1 cup fresh spinach, chopped
- 1/2 cup fresh parsley, chopped
- 1/4 cup green onions, chopped
- 1/4 cup celery, finely chopped
- 2 cloves garlic, minced
- 1/2 cup unsalted butter
- 1/4 cup Pernod or anise-flavored liqueur
- 1/4 cup breadcrumbs
- 1/4 cup grated Parmesan cheese
- Salt and black pepper to taste
- Rock salt or coarse salt for the serving platter
- Lemon wedges for garnish

Instructions

1. Arrange 24 shucked oysters on a baking sheet over rock salt.

2. Sauté spinach, parsley, green onions, celery, and garlic in 1/2 cup butter.

3. Add Pernod, breadcrumbs, Parmesan, salt, and pepper.

4. Spoon the mixture onto oysters.

5. Bake at 450°F for 10-12 mins.

6. Serve on rock salt and garnish with lemon.

Gilded Age (1877-1900)

The Waldorf Salad

The Waldorf Salad, a classic American dish, originated at the Waldorf Hotel (now the Waldorf Astoria) in New York City in the late 19th century. The salad was first created for a charity ball held at the hotel in 1893, and it quickly gained popularity. The original version, devised by maître d'hôtel Oscar Tschirky, consisted of apples, celery, and mayonnaise. Over the years, variations have been introduced, incorporating ingredients such as walnuts, grapes, and raisins.

The Waldorf Salad is renowned for its simple yet elegant combination of crisp apples, crunchy celery, and the creamy dressing. Its popularity endured through the 20th century, becoming a staple in American households and an iconic representation of classic American salads. The Waldorf Salad exemplifies the timeless appeal of dishes that balance contrasting textures and flavors, standing as a testament to the enduring legacy of American culinary creations.

Ingredients

Salad:
- 2 apples, cored and diced
- 1 cup celery, thinly sliced
- 1 cup red grapes, halved
- 1 cup walnuts, chopped
- Fresh lemon juice (for apples)

Dressing:
- 1/2 cup mayonnaise
- 2 tablespoons sour cream
- 1 tablespoon honey
- 1 tablespoon lemon juice
- Salt and pepper to taste

Optional Additions:
- Raisins

Instructions

1. Dice 2 apples and toss with lemon juice.

2. Slice 1 cup celery.

3. Halve 1 cup grapes.

4. Chop 1 cup walnuts.

5. Whisk 1/2 cup mayo, 2 tbsp yogurt, 1 tbsp honey, 1 tbsp lemon juice, salt, and pepper.

6. Combine all ingredients and toss with the dressing.

7. Chill for 30 mins.

Gilded Age (1877-1900)

Chicken à la King

Chicken à la King, a classic dish, has its origins in late 19th to early 20th-century America. The exact origin is debated, with claims attributing it to different chefs and restaurants. However, it gained popularity in the early 20th century as a luxurious and elegant poultry dish.

Typically made with diced chicken in a creamy, savory sauce with mushrooms, bell peppers, and pimentos, Chicken à la King reflects the culinary tastes of the Gilded Age and Progressive Era. Served over rice, pasta, or toast, it became a staple in upscale dining establishments and homes. Its versatility and rich flavor profile made it a favorite for entertaining, showcasing the opulence and creativity of American cuisine during a period of culinary refinement and experimentation. Today, Chicken à la King remains a timeless comfort classic, embodying the enduring appeal of creamy, hearty dishes.

Ingredients

- 2 cups cooked chicken, diced
- 1/4 cup unsalted butter
- 1/4 cup all-purpose flour
- 1/2 teaspoon salt
- 1/4 teaspoon black pepper
- 1/4 teaspoon paprika
- 1 1/2 cups chicken broth
- 1 1/2 cups milk
- 1/2 cup heavy cream
- 1/2 cup green bell pepper, diced
- 1/2 cup red bell pepper, diced
- 1 cup mushrooms, sliced
- 1/4 cup pimentos, chopped
- 2 tablespoons sherry (optional)
- Chopped parsley for garnish
- Cooked rice, pasta, or toast

Instructions

1. Dice 2 cups cooked chicken.

2. In a skillet, melt 1/4 cup butter.

3. Whisk in 1/4 cup flour, salt, pepper, and paprika.

4. Gradually add 1 1/2 cups chicken broth, 1 1/2 cups milk, and 1/2 cup cream.

5. Stir in bell peppers, mushrooms, pimentos. Add chicken.

7. Optional: 2 tbsp sherry.

8. Serve over rice, pasta, or toast.

9. Garnish with parsley.

Gilded Age (1877-1900)

Parker House Rolls

Parker House Rolls trace their origin to the 19th century, specifically to Boston's Parker House Hotel. Created by the hotel's baker, they made their debut in the 1870s. The iconic feature of these buttery, soft rolls is the unique folding technique, originating from an unintentional incident. As the story goes, the baker, seeking a way to mend a mishap in shaping the dough, inadvertently created the distinctive folded form. This accident led to the creation of a beloved bread roll.

Parker House Rolls gained immense popularity and became a staple not just in the hotel but in American households. The recipe was eventually published, and the rolls earned a place on dining tables across the nation. These rolls, with their golden exterior and fluffy interior, encapsulate the charm of timeless, comforting American bread-making traditions.

Ingredients

- 4 cups all-purpose flour
- 1/4 cup granulated sugar
- 1 teaspoon salt
- 2 1/4 teaspoons active dry yeast (1 packet)
- 1 1/2 cups milk, lukewarm
- 1/4 cup unsalted butter, melted
- 1 large egg

For Brushing:
- 1/4 cup unsalted butter, melted

Instructions

1. Activate yeast in lukewarm milk with sugar.

2. Whisk flour and salt. Add melted butter, beaten egg, and yeast mixture.

4. Knead into a smooth dough. Let it rise

6. Roll out, cut rounds, brush with melted butter, and fold.

7. Arrange in a dish and let it rise again.

8. Preheat the oven to 375°F.

9. Bake for 15-20 mins. & Brush with more butter.

11. Serve warm and enjoy the soft, buttery delight of Parker House Rolls!

Gilded Age (1877-1900)

Gumbo Z'Herbes

Gumbo Z'Herbes, deeply embedded in the cultural mosaic of Louisiana, emerged in the Gilded Age as a unique Creole soup. Derived from the French term *"gombo aux herbes"* translating to "okra with greens," this dish exemplifies culinary ingenuity shaped by African, French, and Spanish influences in the region.

Traditionally enjoyed during Lent or as a spring cleanser, Gumbo Z'Herbes boasts a blend of greens—collards, mustard greens, and spinach—symbolizing renewal and abundance. Often incorporating smoked meats, it mirrors the resourcefulness of Creole cooks in maximizing available ingredients.

With its intricate flavors and cultural importance, Gumbo Z'Herbes embodies the vibrant Creole culinary heritage of the Gilded Age South, testifying to the rich amalgamation of diverse culinary traditions that left an enduring mark on American cuisine.

Ingredients

For the Gumbo Base:
- 1 cup vegetable oil
- 1 cup all-purpose flour
- 1 large onion, finely chopped
- 1 bell pepper, finely chopped
- 2 celery stalks, finely chopped
- 4 cloves garlic, minced
- 8 cups vegetable or chicken broth
- 1 bay leaf
- Salt and pepper to taste

For the Greens:
- 1 bunch collard greens, stems removed, chopped
- 1 bunch mustard greens, stems removed, chopped
- 1 bunch turnip greens, stems removed, chopped
- 1 bunch spinach, chopped
- 1 bunch Swiss chard, chopped
- 1/2 cup parsley, chopped

For the Seasonings:
1 teaspoon dried thyme
- 1 teaspoon dried oregano
- 1 teaspoon smoked paprika
- 1/2 teaspoon cayenne pepper (adjust to taste)
- 1/2 teaspoon black pepper

Instructions

1. Make a dark roux.

2. Sauté onion, bell pepper, celery, and garlic. Add broth, bay leaf, salt, and pepper.

4. Integrate collard, mustard, turnip greens, spinach, Swiss chard, and parsley. Season with thyme, oregano, smoked paprika, cayenne, and black pepper.

6. Optionally, add smoked sausage or ham hock. Simmer for 1 hour.

8. Serve over rice.

Gilded Age (1877-1900)

Lobster Newberg

Lobster Newberg, a decadent seafood dish, originated in the Gilded Age, specifically in the late 19th century New York City. The dish is credited to sea captain Ben Wenberg, who frequented Delmonico's, a renowned restaurant of the era. Legend has it that Wenberg, a good friend of restaurant owner Charles Delmonico, shared his recipe with chef Charles Ranhofer.

Originally named Lobster à la Wenberg, the dish featured lobster chunks sautéed in butter, flambéed with brandy, and finished with a rich cream sauce. Due to a feud between Wenberg and Delmonico, the dish was later altered and reintroduced as Lobster Newberg, securing its place on the menu.

Lobster Newberg's popularity soared, becoming a symbol of extravagant dining during the Gilded Age. Despite the historical dispute, the dish continues to epitomize luxury and indulgence in American seafood cuisine.

Ingredients

- 2 lobsters (about 1 to 1.5 pounds each), cooked and meat removed
- 1/2 cup unsalted butter
- 1/2 cup brandy or cognac
- 1 cup heavy cream
- 4 large egg yolks
- Salt and cayenne pepper to taste
- Chopped fresh parsley for garnish

Instructions

1. Begin by steaming the lobsters.
2. Sauté the lobster meat in butter.
3. Add brandy and ignite briefly.
4. Simmer the mixture with cream until slightly thickened.
5. Beat egg yolks and temper them with a small amount of the hot cream mixture.
6. Gradually whisk the tempered yolks into the cream mixture and cook until thickened.
7. Season with salt and cayenne.
8. Return the lobster to the skillet, gently reheating in the sauce.
9. Garnish with chopped parsley.
10. Serve over toast points or buttered toast.

Gilded Age (1877-1900)

The Bourbon Hot Brown

The Hot Brown sandwich, created at the Brown Hotel in Louisville, Kentucky, in the 1920s, emerged at the tail end of the Gilded Age. While it may not have direct ties to the culinary practices of the Gilded Age itself, it can be seen as a product of the evolving American culinary landscape during that period, specifically the rise of grand hotels and fine dining establishments catering to the elite.

Initially a culinary experiment, the Hot Brown swiftly gained acclaim and became a signature dish at the Brown Hotel. Over the years, it has transcended its origin, turning into a beloved comfort food emblematic of Kentucky's culinary heritage. Today, the Hot Brown remains a cherished part of Southern cuisine, celebrated for its hearty and flavorful combination.

Ingredients

For the Mornay Sauce:
- 2 tablespoons unsalted butter
- 2 tablespoons all-purpose flour
- 1 1/2 cups whole milk
- 1/2 cup grated Parmesan cheese
- 1/2 cup Gruyere or Swiss cheese, shredded
- 1/4 cup bourbon
- Salt and pepper to taste

For the Sandwich:
- Sliced roast turkey
- Crispy bacon strips
- Sliced fresh tomatoes
- Thick slices of bread (traditionally Texas toast)

Instructions

1. Melt butter in a saucepan.

2. Stir in flour to form a smooth roux.

3. Whisk in milk until the mixture thickens.

4. Add Parmesan, salt, and pepper.

5. Stir in a generous splash of bourbon.

6. Assemble the Hot Brown sandwich by layering turkey, bacon, and tomatoes on bread.

7. Pour the bourbon-infused Mornay sauce generously over the sandwich.

8. Broil until golden.

9. Garnish with additional Parmesan, a sprinkle of paprika, and fresh parsley.

Gilded Age (1877-1900)

Turkey Tetrazzini with Brandy

Turkey Tetrazzini, a beloved American pasta dish, traces its roots to the early 20th century. Named in honor of Italian opera singer Luisa Tetrazzini, whoes peak years as a singer started in the 1890s, it is said to have been created by chef Ernest Arbogast. The dish features diced turkey meat, mushrooms, and spaghetti enveloped in a creamy sauce made with broth, cream, and Parmesan cheese.

First introduced in the Palace Hotel in San Francisco, where Tetrazzini was a frequent guest, this indulgent creation quickly gained popularity. Its association with opulence and comfort made it a classic choice for re-purposing Thanksgiving leftovers, especially turkey.

Turkey Tetrazzini's enduring appeal lies in its rich flavors and adaptability, embodying the spirit of inventive American cuisine in the early 1900s. Today, it remains a comforting dish, celebrated for its delicious blend of pasta, poultry, and creamy goodness. We might be a few years off on this one as well, but it is a favourite at my home.

Ingredients

- 8 oz spaghetti, cooked *al dente*
- 2 cups cooked turkey, diced
- 1 cup mushrooms, sliced
- 1/2 cup unsalted butter
- 1/2 cup all-purpose flour
- 2 cups turkey or chicken broth
- 1 cup heavy cream
- 1/4 cup brandy
- 1 cup Parmesan cheese, grated
- Salt and black pepper to taste
- 1/2 cup fresh parsley, chopped
- Grated nutmeg for garnish (optional)

Instructions

1. Cook spaghetti.
2. Dice turkey and slice mushrooms.
3. Melt butter, add flour for a roux.
4. Whisk in broth, cream, and brandy.
5. Simmer, add Parmesan, salt, and pepper.
6. Combine with turkey, mushrooms, and spaghetti.
7. Transfer to a baking dish.
8. Bake until golden.
9. Garnish with parsley and nutmeg.

Gilded Age (1877-1900)

Boston Creme Pie

Boston Cream Pie, an iconic American dessert, has its roots in the 19th century at the Parker House Hotel in Boston, Massachusetts, around 1856. Originally named "Chocolate Cream Pie," it was later dubbed "Boston Cream Pie," likely due to its popularity in the city. Created by the hotel's French chef, M. Sanzian, the original version featured two layers of sponge cake filled with pastry cream and topped with chocolate glaze. The Omni Parker House proudly claims it as a signature dish. Evolving over the years, this classic dessert is cherished for its blend of moist cake, velvety custard, and decadent chocolate, remaining a beloved treat in American culinary culture. Today, Boston Cream Pie endures as a beloved American treat, celebrated for its delightful blend of moist cake, velvety custard, and decadent chocolate. Its legacy persists at the Omni Parker House, where it originated, and the dessert continues to inspire reinterpretations in the diverse landscape of American culinary delights.

Ingredients

Sponge Cake:
1 cup all-purpose flour
1 teaspoon baking powder
1/4 teaspoon salt
4 large eggs
1 cup granulated sugar
1 teaspoon vanilla extract
1/2 cup whole milk
1/4 cup unsalted butter, melted

Pastry Cream Filling:
2 cups whole milk
1/2 cup granulated sugar
1/4 cup cornstarch
1/4 teaspoon salt
4 large egg yolks
2 tablespoons unsalted butter
1 teaspoon vanilla extract

Chocolate Ganache:
1/2 cup heavy cream
1 cup semisweet or bittersweet chocolate, chopped
2 tablespoons unsalted butter

Instructions

1. Sponge Cake: Preheat oven to 350°F (175°C). Mix dry ingredients. Beat eggs, sugar; add vanilla, milk, melted butter. Pour into greased pans. Bake for 25-30 mins or until a toothpick comes out clean.

2. Pastry Cream: Whisk sugar, cornstarch, salt, yolks. Heat milk; add to mixture. Cook until thick. Stir in butter, vanilla.

3. Chocolate Ganache: Heat cream, pour over chocolate and butter. Stir until smooth.

4. Assembly: Layer cake, add pastry cream. Top with second layer, pour ganache. Chill. Garnish with whipped cream, chocolate shavings.

Gilded Age (1877-1900)

Chicken & Waffles

Chicken and waffles, a culinary gem with roots in the Gilded Age, marries savory and sweet elements in a harmonious symphony of flavors and textures. Emerging in the early 20th century, the dish's origins intertwine with Southern and African American cuisines, echoing the opulence and diverse influences of the Gilded Age.

While its fame blossomed in Harlem, New York's jazz clubs, the dish's essence can be traced back to the South, reflecting the era's blend of cultural influences. This indulgent pairing of crispy fried chicken and fluffy waffles epitomizes the Gilded Age's penchant for extravagant and diverse culinary experiences. The dish, now celebrated across the United States, serves as a delectable reminder of the cultural richness and culinary innovations that characterized the Gilded Age's dining landscape.

Ingredients

For the Fried Chicken:
- Chicken pieces (legs, thighs, or wings)
- Buttermilk
- All-purpose flour
- Cornstarch
- Salt and pepper
- Paprika
- Garlic powder
- Onion powder
- Cayenne pepper (optional for heat)
- Vegetable oil for frying

For the Waffles:
- All-purpose flour
- Baking powder
- Salt
- Sugar
- Eggs
- Milk
- Unsalted butter (melted)
- Vanilla extract

Instructions

1. Marinate chicken for up to 24 hours in buttermilk.

2. Coat with a mix of flour and spices then Fry until golden, maintaining oil temperature between 350°F to 375°F (175°C to 190°C).

For the waffles:
3. Blend flour, baking powder, salt, sugar, eggs, milk, melted butter, and vanilla. Cook until golden.

4. Assemble by placing crispy chicken on fluffy waffles. Drizzle with syrup.

Progressive Era (1900-1920)

Sam Wo's Wonton Soup

Established in 1907, Sam Wo in the heart of San Francisco's Chinatown was a culinary haven, celebrated for its exquisite Wonton Soup. A testament to Chinese-American culinary tradition, the dish featured meticulously crafted wontons filled with a delectable blend of seasoned pork or shrimp. Nestled in a fragrant chicken or pork-based broth, the dumplings were accompanied by slender egg noodles, providing a delightful interplay of textures. Adorned with aromatic hints of ginger and scallions, the soup showcased the restaurant's culinary finesse, creating a harmonious symphony of flavors. Sam Wo, with its historic charm and legendary dishes, including the iconic Wonton Soup, stood as a revered landmark in San Francisco's vibrant culinary tapestry since its inception over a century ago.

Ingredients

For Wontons:
- 1/2 pound ground pork or shrimp (or a combination)
- 1 cup finely chopped Napa cabbage
- 2 green onions, finely chopped
- 1 tablespoon soy sauce
- 1 tablespoon oyster sauce
- 1 teaspoon sesame oil
- 1/2 teaspoon grated ginger
- 1 package wonton wrappers

For Broth:
- 6 cups Chinese Double Broth
- 1 tablespoon soy sauce
- 1 tablespoon rice vinegar
- 1 teaspoon sesame oil
- Salt and white pepper to taste

Optional Garnishes:
- Sliced green onions
- Chopped cilantro
- Sesame seeds

Instructions

For Broth:
1. Simmer 2-3 lbs of chicken and 1-2 lbs of pork bones with aromatics.
2. Use this broth for boiling another chicken to achieve a rich and layered flavor. This process helps intensify the broth's depth.

For Soup:
3. Combine ground pork, cabbage, green onions, soy sauce, oyster sauce, sesame oil, and ginger.
4. Spoon onto wonton wrappers, fold, and seal with water and fingertips.
5. Boil until cooked.
6. In a separate pot, simmer broth with soy sauce, rice vinegar, sesame oil, salt, and white pepper.
7. Ladle broth over cooked wontons & Garnish with green onions and cilantro.

Progressive Era (1900-1920)

Coca-Cola Salad

Invented around 1886 by pharmacist Dr. John Stith Pemberton in Atlanta, Georgia, Coca-Cola originated as a medicinal beverage. Asa Griggs Candler acquired the formula in 1892, establishing The Coca-Cola Company in 1893. The original concoction included coca leaf extract and kola nut. Over time, the formula evolved, and Coca-Cola became an iconic global brand by the early 20th century.

Decades later, in the mid-20th century, creative culinary enthusiasts embraced the soda's versatility. Coca-Cola Salad, a gelatin concoction featuring the iconic beverage, emerged during this period. While its exact origin date is unclear, this salad became a quirky and beloved addition to mid-century American cuisine, showcasing the enduring influence of Coca-Cola on culinary creativity. While including this recipe in the Progressive Era might be a bit of an anachronism, we beg your indulgence for placing it close to the date of coca-cola's birth.

Ingredients

- 2 cups Coca-Cola
- 1 box (3 ounces) flavored gelatin (lime or cherry)
- 1 cup boiling water
- 1 can (20 ounces) crushed pineapple, undrained
- 1 cup maraschino cherries, halved
- 1 cup chopped nuts (optional)
- Whipped cream or vanilla ice cream for serving (optional)

Instructions

1. Dissolve lime or cherry gelatin in 1 cup boiling water.

2. Add 2 cups Coca-Cola.

3. Refrigerate until partially set.

4. Stir in crushed pineapple, halved cherries, and nuts.

5. Pour into a mold.

6. Chill until fully set.

7. Serve on its own or with whipped cream.

Progressive Era (1900-1920)

Elevated Chicken à la Maryland

Chicken à la Maryland, originating in 19th-century Maryland, reflects the progressive culinary trends of the Progressive Era in the United States. This period, marked by social and cultural changes, saw a shift in cooking techniques and a fusion of regional flavors. Chicken à la Maryland's pan-frying method aligns with the era's interest in culinary innovation and modern techniques. The dish, with its roots in Southern cuisine, exemplifies the Progressive Era's embrace of culinary fusion and the blending of diverse flavors. As transportation and distribution networks improved, the era witnessed increased access to a variety of ingredients, contributing to the dish's popularity. With its indulgent preparation and rich cream gravy, Chicken à la Maryland symbolizes the Progressive Era's fascination with luxury and elaborate culinary creations, making it a fitting inclusion in a this section of our small book.

Ingredients

- 4 bone-in, skin-on chicken thighs
- Salt and pepper to taste
- 1 cup buttermilk
- 1 cup seasoned flour (include herbs and spices)
- 3 tablespoons clarified butter
- 2 tablespoons duck fat
- 1 cup wild mushroom medley
- 1/2 cup dry white wine
- 1 cup heavy cream
- 1/2 cup chicken stock
- Fresh thyme and chives for garnish

Instructions

1. Marinate chicken for up to 24 hours in buttermilk.

2. Dredge in seasoned flour.

3. Pan-fry in clarified butter and duck fat until golden.

4. Finish in the oven at 375°F (190°C) for approx 20 minutes.

For the Sauce:
5. Sauté wild mushrooms.

6. Deglaze with white wine.

7. Add cream and chicken stock.

8. Simmer for a rich sauce.

9. Plate chicken on a mushroom bed.

10. Garnish with fresh herbs.

Progressive Era (1900-1920)

Sloppy Joe

Between 1900-1920, the proto-Sloppy Joe, a precursor to the modern version, emerged as loose-meat sandwiches, gaining popularity in early diners and cafés. Featuring seasoned ground meat, often beef, on a bun, these sandwiches were flavored with simple spices, lacking the distinctive tomato-based sauce of later Sloppy Joes. Affordable, easy to prepare, and satisfying, they became a staple in diners during the era's proliferation of lunch counters. The proto-Sloppy Joe laid the foundation for the evolution of the dish into the saucy, iconic Sloppy Joe recognized today. Born in the 1930s, the modern Sloppy Joe, with ground meat and a tomato-based sauce, likely originated in the 1940s. Named possibly after a Key West bar, Sloppy Joes became a Great Depression staple, evolving into a classic American casual dining dish with delicious variations.

Ingredients

- 1 lb ground beef
- 1 onion, finely chopped
- 1 bell pepper, finely chopped
- 2 cloves garlic, minced
- 1 cup homemade ketchup
- 1 tablespoon brown sugar
- 1 tablespoon Worcestershire sauce
- 1 teaspoon mustard
- Salt and pepper to taste
- Hamburger buns

Instructions

1. Brown ground beef.

2. Sauté onion, bell pepper, and garlic.

3. Add homemade ketchup, brown sugar, Worcestershire sauce, and mustard.

4. Simmer for flavor.

5. Spoon onto toasted buns.

Variation
Maple-Bacon Joe

Cook diced bacon until crispy and fold it into the simmering Sloppy Joes. Finish with a drizzle of maple syrup for a sweet and savory delight.

Progressive Era (1900-1920)

Homemade Ketchup

In the early 1900s, homemade ketchup was a staple as commercial versions gained popularity. Households often crafted ketchup using tomatoes, vinegar, sugar, and spices, adapting recipes from family traditions. The era saw increased industrialization, influencing the transition from homemade to store-bought products. With the rise of convenience foods, commercial ketchup brands gained prominence. Despite this shift, many families continued to prepare ketchup at home, preserving culinary heritage. The homemade process allowed for customization, reflecting regional tastes and preferences. By the mid-20th century, while commercial ketchup dominated the market, the practice of making homemade ketchup persisted, showcasing a blend of tradition and adaptation in American kitchens during this period in food culture.

Ingredients

- 2 cans (28 ounces each) crushed tomatoes
- 1 cup white vinegar
- 1 cup brown sugar
- 1 teaspoon onion powder
- 1 teaspoon garlic powder
- 1 teaspoon mustard powder
- 1 teaspoon salt
- 1/2 teaspoon ground black pepper
- 1/4 teaspoon ground cloves
- 1/4 teaspoon allspice
- 1/4 teaspoon cinnamon

Instructions

1. Simmer crushed tomatoes, vinegar, and brown sugar.

2. Add spices: onion & garlic powder, mustard, salt, pepper, cloves, allspice, and cinnamon.

3. Cook until thick.

4. Cool and refrigerate.

Straining the recipe depends on your preference for texture. If you prefer a smoother consistency, you can strain the mixture after simmering to remove any solids, creating a more refined sauce. If you enjoy a chunkier texture with bits of spices, you can leave it unstrained.

Progressive Era (1900-1920)

Homemade Dried Chipped Beef & Creamed Chipped Beef

In the early 1900s, dried chipped beef became a practical and staple food, especially during wartime and economic challenges. Creamed Chipped Beef, a simple and satisfying dish, gained popularity in American households. Our homemade version pays tribute to that time, combining convenience with a creamy sauce. This dish reflects the culinary landscape of the early 1900s, where practicality met flavor. Recreating Creamed Chipped Beef offers a taste of history, connecting us to the enduring appeal of dishes born out of necessity and adapted for everyday enjoyment.

Pro Tips: Place the beef in the freezer for about 30 minutes to an hour before slicing. This helps firm up the meat, making it easier to achieve thin, even slices. Use a sharp knife like a slicing, carving, or chef's knife. Slice against the grain for tenderness. Hold the knife at a slight 45-degree angle for thinner slices. Or, use a meat slicer.

Ingredients

- 1 pound beef sirloin or round steak
- 1/4 cup kosher salt
- 2 tablespoons brown sugar
- 2 teaspoons black pepper
- 1 teaspoon onion powder
- 1 teaspoon garlic powder
- 1 teaspoon paprika

Instructions

For Preparing Beef for Chipped Beef on Toast:
1. Slice beef thinly.

2. Brine with salt, sugar, pepper, onion and garlic powder, and paprika for 24-48 hrs.

3. Pat dry.

4. Air dry 24-48 hrs in a sterile environment;

or, oven dry at 140-160°F, door slightly ajar; check for doneness, ensure internal temp reaches 160°F;

or, use dehydrator, set at 145°F (63°C), for 4-8 set at hours until desired dryness.

5. Store in the fridge.

For Creamed Chipped Beef:
7. In a pan, sauté 1 cup dried chipped beef.

8. Add 4 tbsp butter, 4 tbsp flour; stir.

9. Pour in 2 cups milk, sprinkle with pepper.

10. Stir until thickened.

11. Serve over toast.

Progressive Era (1900-1920)

Cauliflower Chicken Divan

Chicken Divan, a classic American casserole, has roots in early 20th-century culinary history. Created at the Divan Parisien Restaurant in New York City, the dish gained popularity in the 1930s. It was a collaborative effort between chef Lagasi and socialite Lady Friend, who named it after the restaurant. The original recipe featured broccoli, chicken, and a Mornay sauce, offering a sophisticated twist on comfort food. Widely embraced for its delicious blend of flavors, Chicken Divan became a staple in American households, epitomizing the era's fondness for elegant yet accessible dishes. Its enduring appeal reflects a culinary journey from a notable New York eatery to becoming a beloved comfort dish, showcasing the adaptability and innovation within American cuisine. I personally dislike broccoli, so I am substituting cauliflower, for a broader appeal, though I would not rule out spinach (wilted) or blanched asparagus as noble, elevated substitutions.

Ingredients

- 2 lbs boneless, skinless chicken breasts, cooked and shredded
- 1 large head of cauliflower, cut into florets and steamed
- 1 cup mayonnaise
- 1 cup sour cream
- 1 can (10.75 oz) condensed cream of chicken soup
- 1 cup shredded cheddar cheese
- 1 tablespoon lemon juice
- 1 teaspoon curry powder
- Salt and pepper to taste
- 1 cup breadcrumbs
- 1/4 cup melted butter

Instructions

1. Layer cooked, shredded chicken and steamed cauliflower in a baking dish.

2. Mix mayo, sour cream, cream of chicken soup, cheddar, lemon juice, curry powder, salt, and pepper.

3. Pour the mixture over the chicken and cauliflower.

4. Top with a mixture of breadcrumbs and melted butter.

5. Bake at 350°F (175°C) for 30-35 mins until golden.

Progressive Era (1900-1920)

Potato Kugel

The Potato Kugel recipe reflects the culinary heritage of Jewish immigrants in America during the early 20th century. Arriving with a rich tapestry of traditions, they adapted beloved recipes to suit local ingredients and tastes. Potato Kugel, a comforting casserole, showcased resourcefulness, using readily available potatoes and simple pantry staples. Popularized in Jewish households, it became a cherished dish, embodying a blend of Old World flavors and New World accessibility. Passed down through generations, this dish symbolizes the cultural continuity and culinary adaptation of Jewish communities during an era of immigration and assimilation. Its enduring presence on tables tells a story of resilience, community, and the evolving palate of Jewish-American cuisine in the early 1900s.

Ingredients

- 6 large potatoes, grated
- 1 large onion, grated
- 4 eggs, beaten
- 1/2 cup matzo meal or breadcrumbs
- 1/2 cup schmaltz (rendered chicken fat)
- Salt and pepper to taste

Instructions

1. Grate 6 potatoes and 1 onion; squeeze out excess liquid.

2. Mix with 4 beaten eggs, 1/2 cup matzo meal, and 1/2 cup schmaltz.

3. Add salt and pepper.

4. Grease a baking dish.

5. Bake at 375°F (190°C) for about 1 hour until golden brown.

Variation
Add 1/4 cup each of chopped parsley, dill, and chives to grated potatoes for an herb-infused elegance in your kugel. Adjust to taste.

Progressive Era (1900-1920)

Crabmeat Corn Chowder

Corn chowder, a beloved American dish, has a rich history dating back to the late 19th and early 20th centuries. Its origins can be traced to the United States, where it gained popularity as a comforting and hearty soup, particularly in the Midwestern and Southern regions, where corn was a staple crop. The dish's early iterations were simple and utilized the abundant corn harvests of the time. Recipes for corn chowder can be found as far back as 1884, with variations emerging in various cookbooks across the country. During the 1900-1920 era, corn chowder continued to evolve, with some recipes incorporating cream, milk, or condensed milk, as well as thickeners such as flour or eggs. The dish's enduring appeal and adaptability have cemented its status as a classic American comfort food, cherished for its rich history and delicious, heartwarming flavors.

Ingredients

- 3 cups corn kernels, scraped fresh from the cob, or frozen kernels
- 8 ounces cooked lump crab meat
- 1 tablespoon extra-virgin olive oil
- 2 tablespoons butter
- 2 all-purpose potatoes, peeled and diced
- 2 ribs celery, chopped
- 1 medium yellow onion, chopped
- 1 small red bell pepper, seeded and diced
- 1 bay leaf, fresh or dried
- Salt and freshly ground black pepper
- 1 tablespoon Old Bay seasoning blend
- 3 tablespoons all-purpose flour
- 2 cups vegetable or chicken stock or broth
- 1 quart whole milk
- 1 cup heavy whipping cream
- 1/4 teaspoon kosher salt
- 1/4 teaspoon black pepper
- Oyster crackers for garnish

Instructions

1. In a mix of olive oil and butter, sauté potatoes, celery, onion, and red pepper until tender.

2. Add bay leaf, Old Bay seasoning, and flour; cook for 3 minutes.

3. Pour in vegetable or chicken stock, whole milk, and heavy whipping cream; simmer for 15 minutes.

4. Introduce corn kernels and lump crab meat; cook for an additional 5 minutes.

5. Season the chowder with salt and pepper to taste.

6. Discard the bay leaf and ladle the corn chowder into bowls.

7. Garnish with oyster crackers before serving.

Progressive Era (1900-1920)

Green Banana Molasses Bread

In the early 20th century, the American culinary scene underwent a transformative shift with the incorporation of bananas as a staple ingredient. The United Fruit Company, now Chiquita, played a pivotal role in this change by promoting the exotic fruit's nutritional value and versatility through educational materials and cookbooks. The 1923 "Selected Banana Recipes" cookbook featured an innovative banana bread recipe using green bananas, fat, dark molasses, and yeast, differing from today's quickbread versions. This original recipe draws inspiration from the Franklin Golden Syrup Recipes book and Chiquita's 1923 promotional materials, honoring the era's creative ingredient use. Reflecting a time when bananas evolved from a raw fruit to a culinary staple, this recipe showcases the past's depth of flavor and culinary exploration, blending available ingredients with innovative experiences.

Ingredients

- 2 green bananas
- 1/2 cup dark molasses
- 2 cups all-purpose flour
- 1/2 cup unsalted butter, softened
- 1/2 cup granulated sugar
- 2 large eggs
- 1 teaspoon baking soda
- 1/2 teaspoon salt
- 1 packet (about 2 1/4 teaspoons) active dry yeast
- 1/2 cup warm water (about 110°F/43°C)
- 1 teaspoon vanilla extract

Instructions

1. Mash 2 green bananas.

2. Dissolve 2 1/4 tsp yeast in 1/2 cup warm water.

3. Cream 1/2 cup butter with 1/2 cup sugar; add 2 eggs, mashed bananas, 1/2 cup molasses, and 1 tsp vanilla.

4. Mix 2 cups flour, 1 tsp baking soda, and 1/2 tsp salt.

5. Combine all ingredients.

6. Pour into a loaf pan and let it rise for 1 hour.

7. Bake at 350°F for 60 minutes.

8. Cool before serving.

Roaring Twenties (1920-1929)

Green Goddess Salad

The Green Goddess Salad, a culinary icon, traces its roots to the early 20th century, specifically the Palace Hotel in San Francisco. Created in the 1920s by the hotel's executive chef, Philip Roemer, the salad was a homage to actor George Arliss and his hit play "The Green Goddess." Its vibrant green dressing, made with mayonnaise, sour cream, chives, tarragon, and anchovies, captivated diners' palates. The salad quickly gained popularity, becoming a symbol of culinary sophistication. Over the years, variations emerged, but the essence of the Green Goddess Salad, with its lush, herb-infused dressing, continues to be a beloved classic, showcasing the enduring influence of creative chefs and the fusion of theater and gastronomy in American culinary history. Our version maintains the harmony of flavors while offering a milder onion presence.

Ingredients

For the Dressing:
- 1 cup mayonnaise
- 1 cup sour cream
- 1/4 cup fresh parsley, chopped
- 2 tablespoons fresh chives, chopped
- 2 tablespoons fresh tarragon, chopped
- 2 anchovy fillets, minced
- 1 clove garlic, minced
- 2 tablespoons white wine vinegar
- Salt and pepper to taste

For the Salad:
- Mixed salad greens (lettuce, spinach, arugula, etc.)
- Cherry tomatoes, halved
- Cucumber, sliced
- Avocado, diced
- Radishes, thinly sliced
- Sweet onion or green onions (scallions), thinly sliced

Instructions

1. Blend mayo, sour cream, parsley, chives, tarragon, anchovies, garlic, vinegar, salt, and pepper for the Green Goddess dressing.

2. In a bowl, combine mixed greens, cherry tomatoes, cucumber, avocado, radishes, and sweet onion or green onions.

3. Drizzle with the dressing.

4. Toss gently and serve.

Roaring Twenties (1920-1929)

Hay & Straw

In the 1920s, the culinary landscape in the U.S. underwent a significant paradigm shift with the introduction of frozen foods, notably frozen peas, a breakthrough pioneered by Clarence Birdseye, the "Captain of Cold." His experiments revealed that blanching and fast-freezing peas immediately after picking preserved their flavor and texture. By 1929, the Birds Eye company was freezing and storing various foods, launching a major campaign to introduce the luxury of enjoying fresh-tasting vegetables and seafood out of season. However, the necessary infrastructure for the frozen food industry's success emerged post-World War II. Birdseye's fast freezing techniques revolutionized food availability, allowing year-round enjoyment of diverse foods. Simultaneously, the 1920s saw significant growth and innovation in the ham industry, . Canned and fully cooked ham products became popular in quick and easy recipes like the colorful "Hay and Straw" pasta dish, reflecting the era's convenience-focused culinary trends.

Ingredients

- 2 cups julienned fully cooked ham
- 3 cups frozen peas
- 1 package (16 ounces) linguine, 1 tablespoon butter
- 1 1/2 cups shredded Parmesan cheese.

Instructions

1. Cook linguine according to package directions.

2. In a large skillet, sauté ham in butter until heated through.

3. Stir in peas; cook, covered, until heated through.

4. Drain linguine.

5. Toss linguine with ham mixture and cheese.

Variation
Blue Cheese Alfredo

1. Melt 1/2 cup butter, whisk in 1 cup heavy cream, and stir in 1 1/2 cups grated Parmesan with a pinch of nutmeg for a quick Alfredo sauce. Adjust to taste.

2. Blend crumbled blue cheese into the Alfredo sauce for a tangy, creamy twist. Toss with linguine, ham, and peas. Indulge in bold flavors!

Roaring Twenties (1920-1929)

Ambrosia Salad

Ambrosia salad, a delightful and fruity dish, has its roots in the late 19th-century southern United States. The term "ambrosia" evokes the food of the gods in Greek mythology, capturing the heavenly taste of this salad. Early recipes combined fresh citrus fruits, coconut, and sometimes marshmallows, offering a light and refreshing dessert.

Gaining popularity in the early to mid-20th century, ambrosia evolved with regional variations and the addition of ingredients like canned fruit, whipped cream, and mini marshmallows. By the 1950s, it became a potluck and holiday staple, symbolizing Southern hospitality. The enduring appeal lies in its harmonious blend of sweet and citrus flavors, making it a timeless classic gracing tables during festive occasions, a delightful reminder of culinary traditions passed through generations.

Instant pudding mix, introduced by My-T-Fine in 1918 and later by Jell-O in the 1930s, became a versatile pantry staple, revolutionizing dessert preparation for over half a century.

Ingredients

- 1 cup mandarin oranges, drained
- 1 cup pineapple chunks, drained
- 1 cup shredded coconut
- 1 cup mini marshmallows
- 1 cup whipped cream or whipped topping
- 1 cup vanilla pudding (prepared from Instant Pudding Mix)
- Maraschino cherries for garnish (optional)

Instructions

1. Combine oranges, pineapple, coconut, and marshmallows.

2. Mix vanilla pudding with whipped cream.

3. Layer fruits and pudding mix in glasses.

4. Chill for 1 hour.

5. Garnish with cherries.

Roaring Twenties (1920-1929)

Wonder Bread

Wonder Bread, introduced in 1921 by Taggart Baking Company, revolutionized the American bread industry. Its creation was prompted by advancements in a process that aerated bread, creating a soft texture. This marked the birth of sliced bread, with Wonder Bread becoming synonymous with the convenience of pre-sliced loaves. The brand's iconic red, yellow, and blue logo became a staple on grocery shelves. Wonder Bread gained popularity for its consistent quality and freshness. Over the years, it navigated through ownership changes and market shifts. Despite facing criticism for nutritional content, it remained a household name, reflecting the evolution of American eating habits. The phrase "the greatest thing since sliced bread" highlights its cultural impact, making Wonder Bread a symbol of innovation and convenience in the history of American baking. The following recipe is an homage to this iconic brand.

Ingredients

- 4 cups all-purpose flour
- 2 tablespoons sugar
- 1 tablespoon active dry yeast
- 1 1/2 teaspoons salt
- 1 1/4 cups warm milk
- 2 tablespoons unsalted butter, softened

Instructions

1. Combine warm milk, sugar, and yeast.

2. Mix with flour, salt, and softened butter.

3. Knead the dough and let it rise until doubled.

4. Shape the dough and let it rise in a pan.

5. Bake at 375°F for 25-30 minutes.

6. Cool, slice, and savor your homemade "Wonder"Bread!

Roaring Twenties (1920-1929)

Baby Ruth Bars

Baby Ruth bars, introduced in 1921 by the Curtiss Candy Company, have a storied and debated history. Despite the company's claim that the candy was named after President Grover Cleveland's daughter, Ruth, speculation persists that it aimed to capitalize on the fame of baseball legend Babe Ruth. The candy's nougat, caramel, peanuts, and chocolate coating quickly gained popularity, becoming an iconic treat during the Roaring Twenties. The Great Depression solidified its status as an affordable indulgence. Over the years, Baby Ruth bars underwent various ownership changes but maintained their popularity. Their enduring appeal lies in the perfect blend of textures and flavors, creating a nostalgic and beloved confection that has stood the test of time in American candy culture. The following recipe is presented as an homage to this iconic candy bar.

Ingredients

- 1 cup smooth peanut butter
- 1 cup powdered sugar
- 1 cup crushed peanuts
- 1 cup caramel candies, unwrapped
- 2 tablespoons heavy cream
- 2 cups milk chocolate chips
- 2 tablespoons vegetable shortening

Instructions

1. Mix peanut butter, powdered sugar, and peanuts.

2. Press the mixture into a pan.

3. Melt caramels with cream, pour over the peanut mixture.

4. Allow it to cool.

5. Melt chocolate with shortening, pour on top.

6. Chill for 2 hours.

7. Cut into bars.

Roaring Twenties (1920-1929)

Candy Techniques for Baby Ruth Bars

Crafting homemade Baby Ruth-type Bars requires mastery of specialized candy-making techniques. The process begins with the meticulous preparation of the Caramel Layer, demanding a keen eye for low-heat caramelization. Unwrapped caramel candies are gently heated with precisely measured heavy cream to create a silky, flavorful caramel sauce. Consistent stirring is crucial to achieve the right consistency, ensuring the success of this layer. This skillful process results in a delectable foundation over the peanut layer, enhancing the overall decadence of the bars. The careful execution of each step brings forth the rich flavors and textures that define the indulgent delight of homemade Baby Ruth Bars.

Caramel Layer:

1. Gently heat unwrapped caramel candies with 2 tablespoons of heavy cream in a saucepan over low heat.

2. Stir consistently until the caramels melt and blend with the cream, creating a smooth caramel sauce.

3. Pour the caramel mixture evenly over the peanut layer.

4. Allow it to cool and set before proceeding with the chocolate coating step.

Chocolate Coating:

1. In a microwave-safe bowl, melt the milk chocolate chips with 2 tablespoons of vegetable shortening in 30-second intervals.

2. Stir after each interval until the chocolate is completely melted and smooth.

3. Pour the melted chocolate over the caramel layer.

4. Continue with the chilling process as mentioned in the previous steps.

Roaring Twenties (1920-1929)

Ancient Grain Salmon Pie

During the Roaring Twenties in the U.S., a cultural shift towards convenience and modernity transformed culinary trends. Canned goods symbolized progress and efficiency, riding the wave of innovations in food preservation technologies. Canned salmon, a manifestation of quick, accessible, and versatile food options, gained prominence as a household staple. In the fast-paced lifestyle of the Roaring Twenties, the extended shelf life and ease of use of canned salmon made it a favorite for homemakers seeking efficient ways to prepare nutritious meals. This culinary landscape embraced modernity while preserving traditional flavors.

The Rustic Salmon Pie, inspired by this trend, seamlessly blends canned salmon's convenience with wholesome ingredients. This dish pays homage to the Roaring Twenties, where culinary innovation met the demand for efficient, satisfying gastronomic experiences, reflecting the essence of changing foodways in the early 20th Century.

Ingredients

For the Crust:
- 1 cup spelt flour
- 1 cup whole wheat flour
- 2 teaspoons baking powder
- 1/2 teaspoon salt
- 1/4 cup extra-virgin olive oil
- 1/2 cup buttermilk
- 1 egg

For the Filling:
- 2 Yukon Gold potatoes, diced and boiled
- 1 can (14 oz) canned salmon, drained
- 1/2 cup low-fat plain yogurt
- 1/4 cup buttermilk
- 1/2 cup frozen peas
- 1/2 cup frozen corn
- 2 tablespoons fresh parsley, chopped
- Salt and pepper to taste
- 1 cup sharp cheddar cheese, shredded

Instructions

1. Mix flours, baking powder, salt. Add oil, buttermilk, egg. Roll into a crust.

2. Mix filling ingredients.

3. Pour filling into crust, top with cheddar.

4. Bake at 375°F for 30-35 mins.

5. Cool, slice, and enjoy!

Optional:
Elevate the flavor profile by mixing finely chopped fresh dill and lemon zest into the filling. This combination adds a refreshing and citrusy note that complements the salmon and potatoes.

Roaring Twenties (1920-1929)

Olive Sandwiches & Our Black Olive & Fig on Croissant

In the 1920s, olive sandwiches emerged as a popular and distinctive dish in the United States. Fueled by the economic prosperity of the Roaring Twenties, Americans embraced new culinary trends, and olive sandwiches became a unique addition to social gatherings and tea parties. The simplicity of the recipe, combining cream cheese and chopped green olives, appealed to the era's taste for elegant yet accessible finger foods. Olive sandwiches quickly gained popularity as a fashionable and affordable option for entertaining guests, reflecting the broader cultural shift towards modernity and experimentation. While seemingly unconventional to contemporary palates, these sandwiches exemplify the culinary creativity and adaptability characteristic of the 1920s, a decade marked by evolving social norms and a desire for novel gastronomic experiences. The Classic Olive and Cream Cheese Sandwich is pretty much self-explanatory. Here we are opting for a Fig and Olive Spread, which is more in keeping with contemporary tastes.

Ingredients

- 2 large croissants
- 1/2 cup black olives, chopped
- 2 tablespoons fig jam
- 4 ounces goat cheese
- Handful of arugula
- Salt and pepper to taste

Instructions

1. Pit and chop black olives.

2. Mix chopped olives with fig jam.

3. Slice croissants in half.

4. Spread olive and fig mixture on the bottom half.

5. Add goat cheese.

6. Place arugula on top.

7. Sprinkle salt and pepper.

8. Cover with the top half.

9. Serve immediately. Optionally, warm croissants before assembling.

Roaring Twenties (1920-1929)

Girl Scout Cookies

Girl Scout Cookies have a fascinating history, originating in 1917 when the Mistletoe Troop in Muskogee, Oklahoma, baked and sold cookies in their high school cafeteria. By 1936, the national Girl Scout organization published the first official cookie recipe in its handbook, marking the beginning of a nationwide fundraising tradition. Initially supporting local activities, the proceeds evolved into a vital source of funding. In 1951, commercial bakeries standardized offerings like Thin Mints and Trefoils. The iconic door-to-door sales began in the 1950s, contributing to the cookies' cultural significance. Today, Girl Scout Cookies empower girls, teaching entrepreneurship and funding programs while offering a beloved annual treat that transcends generations. The Classic Thin Mint Cookie, introduced in the 1950s, symbolizes the enduring popularity cultivated during the 1920s. This recipe is presented as an homage to an enduring classic.

Ingredients

- 2 cups all-purpose flour
- 1 cup unsweetened cocoa powder
- 1/4 teaspoon salt
- 1 cup unsalted butter, softened
- 1 cup granulated sugar
- 1 teaspoon vanilla extract
- 1/2 teaspoon peppermint extract
- 8 ounces dark chocolate, chopped
- 1/2 teaspoon vegetable oil
- Peppermint extract (optional, for extra minty flavor)

Instructions

1. Combine 2 cups flour, 1 cup cocoa, and 1/4 tsp salt. Cream 1 cup softened butter, 1 cup sugar, vanilla, and 1/2 tsp peppermint extract. Mix in dry ingredients.

2. Shape dough into logs and chill for 1 hour.

3. Preheat oven to 350°F. Slice dough and bake for 10-12 mins.

4. Allow cookies to cool.

5. Melt 8 oz dark chocolate with 1/2 tsp vegetable oil. Dip cookies and refrigerate to set.

6. Optionally, add peppermint extract to the melted chocolate for extra minty flavor.

Roaring Twenties (1920-1929)

Clams Casino

Clams Casino, a classic appetizer, traces its origins to the early 20th century in the United States. Legend attributes its creation to Julius Keller, a chef at the Narragansett Pier Casino in Rhode Island. Originally, the dish featured clams topped with bacon and breadcrumbs, baked to perfection. Over time, variations emerged, incorporating diverse ingredients such as bell peppers, shallots, garlic, and herbs.

The dish's popularity soared in the 1920s, as it epitomized the era's love for indulgent and flavorful appetizers. Whether served on the half-shell or nestled in a baking dish, Clams Casino became a staple in seafood cuisine. Today, the variations persist, with chefs adding their creative twists to this timeless dish, ensuring its enduring appeal on modern menus and at home gatherings.

Ingredients

- 24 littleneck clams, scrubbed
- 8 slices bacon, cut into small pieces
- 1/2 cup breadcrumbs
- 1/4 cup grated Parmesan cheese
- 3 cloves garlic, minced
- 2 tablespoons fresh parsley, finely chopped
- 2 tablespoons olive oil
- 1 lemon, cut into wedges

Instructions

1. Scrub 24 clams.

2. Cook bacon until crisp; set aside.

3. Sauté garlic and breadcrumbs in bacon drippings in a skillet. Mix with bacon, Parmesan, and parsley.

4. Place the breadcrumb mixture on top of the clams. Bake at 450°F for 10-12 mins.

5. Serve.
   - Serve with lemon wedges.

Variation
Whiskey Maple Clams Casino

After Step 3, brush clams with a mix of whiskey, maple syrup, and a pinch of cayenne. Bake at 450°F for 10-12 mins for a sweet, smoky, and boozy twist. Serve hot.

Roaring Twenties (1920-1929)

Individual Rum-Infused Pineapple Upside-Down Cakes

Yes, Dear Reader, Pineapple Upside-Down Cake is a recipe from the 1920s. The two earliest printings of this recipe were found in a 1924 Seattle charity cookbook and in a 1927 booklet called Aunt Sammy's Radio Recipes, developed by the Bureau of Home Economics, U.S. Department of Agriculture. Additionally, in 1925, the Hawaiian Pineapple Company sponsored a contest calling for pineapple recipes, and it is said that 2,500 of the 60,000 submissions were recipes for pineapple upside-down cake. The company decided to run an ad about the flood of pineapple upside-down cake recipes it had received, which further increased the cake's popularity. Therefore, the 1920s marked the rise of the pineapple upside-down cake as a beloved and enduring dessert in American culinary history.

Ingredients

- 1/4 cup unsalted butter
- 1/2 cup packed brown sugar
- 1-2 tablespoons dark rum
- 6-8 pineapple rings (fresh or canned)
- Maraschino cherries
- 1 cup all-purpose flour
- 1 teaspoon baking powder
- 1/4 teaspoon salt
- 1/4 cup unsalted butter, softened
- 1/2 cup granulated sugar
- 1 large egg
- 1 teaspoon vanilla extract
- 1/2 cup milk
- 2-3 tablespoons dark rum

Instructions

1. Melt butter, add brown sugar and rum in a saucepan. Divide mixture into a greased muffin tin.

2. Place a pineapple ring and a cherry in each well.

3. In a bowl, mix flour, baking powder, and salt. Cream butter and sugar, beat in egg and vanilla. Add dry ingredients and milk, then rum.

4. Divide batter into the tin. Bake at 350°F for 20-25 minutes.

5. Cool for 5 minutes, then invert onto a wire rack.

Roaring Twenties (1920-1929)

Deviled Eggs with Caviar

Deviled eggs have been a staple in the United States since the 1920s, with the earliest American recipe dating back to 1877. Mayonnaise, a key ingredient, was first incorporated in the 1896 version of "The Boston Cooking-School Cook Book" by Fannie Farmer.

In the 1920s, deviled eggs soared in popularity due to their convenience and suitability as finger foods, fitting the era's trend of easy-to-eat, fashionable party dishes at social gatherings and speakeasies. As economic prosperity and social change characterized the Jazz Age, deviled eggs became synonymous with entertainment.

Our recipe adds a touch of luxury to this classic by incorporating caviar, capturing the exuberance of the Jazz Age. Readers can choose from various caviar options to suit budgets and personal tastes, elevating this timeless dish for a sophisticated twist.

Ingredients

- 6 large eggs
- 3 tablespoons mayonnaise
- 2 teaspoons Dijon mustard
- 1/2 teaspoon sweet & mild paprika
- 1/2 teaspoon white wine vinegar
Salt and pepper to taste
- Caviar (options: Osietra Supreme, Hackleback, Salmon roe, Tobiko, White sturgeon caviar)

Instructions

1. Boil, peel, and halve the eggs. Remove yolks and place in a bowl. Push yolks through a fine-meshed sieve into another bowl.

2. Add mayonnaise, Dijon mustard, paprika, white wine vinegar, salt, and pepper to yolks. Mix well and adjust seasoning.

3. Spoon creamy filling into a piping bag with a wide star nozzle.

4. Pipe mixture into egg white halves.

5. Garnish each deviled egg with a small amount of chosen caviar.

Roaring Twenties (1920-1929)

Tomato "Jell-O" Salad

Jell-O, introduced in 1897, gained immense popularity in the 1920s due to economic prosperity, technological advances, and its versatile nature. The era's experimentation with convenience foods like Jell-O was facilitated by improved home refrigeration and gelatin production. Its adaptability to various flavors and compatibility with both sweet and savory dishes appealed to the evolving lifestyles of the 1920s.

Aggressive marketing, including door-to-door sales and creative advertising, positioned Jell-O as a symbol of modernity and sophistication. The 1920s cultural shift saw Jell-O becoming synonymous with festive occasions and social gatherings, aligning with the vibrant lifestyle of the time. By the decade's end, Jell-O had firmly established itself as a household staple, and its popularity continued to grow.

Our Tomato "Jell-O" salad may seem unconventional today, but it was a popular mid-20th-century American dish, showcasing the versatility and creative applications of Jell-O in historical cuisine.

Ingredients

- 1 1/2 cups tomato juice
- 1/2 cup water
- 2 packets unflavored gelatin
- 1/4 cup finely chopped onion
- 2 tablespoons lemon juice
- 1 teaspoon Worcestershire sauce
- 1/2 teaspoon sugar
- 1/2 teaspoon salt
- 1/4 teaspoon black pepper
- 1/4 teaspoon garlic powder
- 1/4 teaspoon smoked paprika
- 1/4 teaspoon dried basil
- 1/4 teaspoon dried oregano

Instructions

1. Bloom the gelatin in water, then dissolve it over low heat.

2. Add tomato juice, onion, lemon juice, Worcestershire sauce, sugar, salt, pepper, garlic powder, smoked paprika, basil, and oregano. Stir to combine.

3. Pour the mixture into individual molds or a large mold.

4. Refrigerate the aspic for at least 4 hours or until set.

Roaring Twenties (1920-1929)

Lemon Pound Cake

Pound cake, a classic dessert with roots dating back to the early 1700s, earned its name from the original recipe that balanced one pound each of flour, sugar, butter, and eggs. By the 1920s, this simple yet rich cake had become a familiar treat in American households, with variations emerging.

Amelia Simmons's 1796 "American Cookery" included the first American pound cake recipe. In the 1920s, bakers started experimenting, introducing flavors like citrus juice and toppings such as melted butter or sugar glazes. The Ritz Carlton lemon pound cake, potentially originating from the hotel's chef or a guest named Elizabeth Dole, gained popularity.

Pound cake recipes continued evolving, with bakers adjusting proportions for lighter textures. In the 20th century, artificial leaveners were incorporated, deviating from the original equal-weight formula, showcasing the enduring adaptability of this beloved dessert.

Ingredients

- 3 cups all-purpose flour
- 1 tablespoon baking powder
- 3/4 teaspoon salt
- 3 cups sugar
- 1 cup unsalted butter, room temperature
- 1/2 cup shortening, room temperature
- 5 large eggs
- 1 cup whole milk
- 6 tablespoons lemon juice
- Zest of 1 lemon

Optional
- *Incorporate 2 tablespoons of poppy seeds into the dry mix for a delightful crunch that complements the lemon flavor., or*
- *substitute 1 cup of flour for almond flour Adding almond flour introduces a subtle nutty richness, enhancing flavor, and yielding a moister, denser texture.*

Instructions

1. Mix 3 cups flour, 1 tbsp baking powder, 3/4 tsp salt.

2. Cream 3 cups sugar, 1 cup butter, 1/2 cup shortening.

3. Add 5 eggs one by one.

4. Alternate dry mix & 1 cup milk into creamed mix.

5. Add 6 tbsp lemon juice, zest of 1 lemon.

6. Bake at 350°F for 55 mins.

The Depression Era (1930s)

Barley, Beer & Cheese Meatloaf

During the Great Depression in the 1930s, meatloaf became a cost-effective dish, utilizing affordable cuts like ground beef and fillers such as breadcrumbs and vegetables. Its adaptability and nutritional value helped families create hearty meals with limited resources, and leftovers could be repurposed. The popularity of meatloaf during the Depression contributed to its enduring place in American culinary culture. In recent times, culinary innovation has brought creative variations, including exotic meat blends, gluten-free options, and plant-based alternatives, reflecting a dynamic culinary landscape where tradition and ingenuity converge in this comforting classic. During the Great Depression, First Lady Eleanor Roosevelt served meatloaf at the White House, emphasizing its affordability and deliciousness as a symbolic gesture to connect with struggling Americans.

Ingredients

- 1 pound ground beef
- 1/2 pound ground pork
- 1 cup cooked barley (cooled)
- 1 cup shredded cheese (cheddar, mozzarella, or your choice)
- 1/2 cup beer (choose a flavorful variety)
- 1/2 cup breadcrumbs
- 1/4 cup finely chopped onions
- 2 cloves garlic, minced
- 2 eggs
- 1/4 cup ketchup
- 2 tablespoons Worcestershire sauce
- Salt and pepper to taste

Instructions

1. Mix 1 lb ground beef, 1/2 lb ground pork, 1 cup cooked barley, 1 cup cheese, 1/2 cup beer, 1/2 cup breadcrumbs, 1/4 cup onions, 2 minced garlic cloves, 2 eggs, 1/4 cup ketchup, 2 tbsp Worcestershire, salt, and pepper.

2. Shape the mixture into a loaf.

3. Bake at 350°F for 1 hour.

4. Allow the loaf to rest before slicing.

5. Enjoy the rich, savory blend of flavors!

Campfire Cast-Iron Stew: White Kidney Bean and Ham Hock

This rustic white kidney bean and ham hock stew embraces the spirit of Depression-era resourcefulness. Inspired by ad-hoc ingredients, this recipe combines outdoor cooking simplicity with a nod to the frugality and ingenuity of the era. While not a historical replication, it captures the essence of a time when making do with what was available and foraging for herbs were essential skills. The ham hock provides economical depth of flavor, while mushrooms and foraged herbs contribute earthy notes. Simmering over an open flame, this stew embodies a timeless connection to outdoor sustenance and inventive cooking, reminiscent of a bygone era where culinary creativity was born out of necessity, yet has found a place in today's appreciation for flavorful, thrifty meals.

Ingredients

- 1 cup dried white kidney beans, soaked overnight
- 1 ham hock
- 1 cup mushrooms, sliced
- Root vegetables (carrots, potatoes, parsnips), diced
- Foraged herbs (wild thyme, rosemary, or other available herbs)
- 1 onion, chopped
- 2 cloves garlic, minced
- Salt and pepper to taste
- Chicken or vegetable broth
- Olive oil for sautéing

Instructions

1. Sauté onions, garlic, and mushrooms.

2. Add ham hock, soaked white kidney beans, diced root veggies, and foraged herbs.

3. Pour broth to cover, bring to a boil, then simmer 2-3 hours until beans and veggies are tender.

4. Season with salt and pepper.

5. Remove ham hock, shred meat, and return it to the stew.

6. Serve hot, garnished with fresh herbs.

The Depression Era (1930s)

Hobo Bread

The tradition of infusing liquor and dried fruits into bread spans centuries, often tied to celebrations. Born from culinary creativity, this practice endured the hardships of the Depression era, marked by economic struggle. The Hobo Bread recipe pays homage to this flavorful legacy, embracing the practicality of incorporating rum-soaked dried fruits, molasses, and black treacle. In times of scarcity, individuals exhibited ingenuity, crafting resourceful dishes with minimal resources. Baking this dark and hearty bread in a coffee can mirrors the pragmatic approach of train-hoppers, creating meals that were both filling and memorable. Each slice becomes a narrative, connecting the historical tradition of flavorful bread to the resilience, resourcefulness, and communal spirit of Depression-era cooking.

Ingredients

- 2 cups all-purpose flour
- 1 cup whole wheat flour
- 1 cup dark brown sugar
- 1 teaspoon baking soda
- 1 teaspoon baking powder
- 1 teaspoon salt
- 1 teaspoon cinnamon
- 1/2 teaspoon nutmeg
- 1/2 cup molasses or black treacle
- 2/3 cup dark rum or brandy
- 1/2 cup buttermilk
- 1/2 cup vegetable oil
- 2 large eggs
- 1 cup mixed dried fruit (raisins, currants, chopped dates)
- Butter or oil for greasing the coffee can

Instructions

1. Soak dried fruit in rum.

2. Mix flours, sugar, baking soda, and spices.

3. In another bowl, combine molasses, buttermilk, oil, and eggs.

4. Stir the wet ingredients into the dry ingredients.

5. Add the soaked fruit to the mixture.

6. Pour the batter into a greased coffee can.

7. Bake at 350°F for 60-70 minutes.

8. Cool and slice.

The Depression Era (1930s)

Depression Green Chili Stew

During the Depression era, Green Chili Stew emerged as a comforting and economical dish, rooted in the flavors of the American Southwest. Combining local ingredients such as pork, green chilies, and simple spices, this stew embodied the resourcefulness of the time. Families facing economic hardship turned to hearty and affordable meals, and Green Chili Stew offered a flavorful escape from the challenges of the era. The stew's appeal lay in its simplicity and the ability to stretch ingredients, providing sustenance and warmth. Served over rice or with a side of cornbread, it became a symbol of resilience, embodying the spirit of making the most out of what was available. As people sought solace in nourishing meals, Green Chili Stew stood out as a humble yet delicious creation, offering a taste of the Southwest amid the struggles of the Depression.

Ingredients

- 2 pounds pork shoulder, cut into cubes
- 8–10 medium-sized roasted Hatch green chilies, peeled and chopped
- 1 large yellow onion, finely diced
- 5 cloves garlic, minced
- 2 medium-sized potatoes, peeled and diced
- 4 cups rich pork or chicken broth
- 1 teaspoon ground cumin
- 1 teaspoon smoked paprika
- 1/2 teaspoon dried oregano
- 1/2 teaspoon coriander
- 1/4 teaspoon cayenne pepper
- Salt and black pepper to taste
- 2 tablespoons vegetable oil
- Fresh cilantro and lime wedges for garnish

Instructions

1. Sear pork cubes; sauté onions and garlic.

2. Add cumin, smoked paprika, oregano, coriander, and cayenne.

3. Stir in roasted Hatch chilies, potatoes, and broth.

4. Simmer covered until pork is tender (1.5–2 hours).

5. Season with salt and black pepper.

6. Serve hot, garnished with cilantro and lime.

Hatch chilis are New Mexican peppers known for their smoky, mild heat. Substitute with Anaheim or poblano peppers.

The Depression Era (1930s)

Chicago-Style Hot Dog

The Chicago-style hot dog, an iconic culinary creation, has roots tracing back to the Great Depression. As economic hardships prevailed, street vendors in Chicago devised a hearty yet affordable hot dog, providing a flavorful and satisfying meal for a nickel. The Depression-era context influenced the dog's design, featuring a poppy seed bun, an all-beef frankfurter, and a distinctive array of toppings. The city's diverse communities contributed to the toppings, including yellow mustard, chopped onions, neon-green relish, tomato slices, pickles, sport peppers, and a sprinkle of celery salt. This culinary innovation not only catered to limited budgets but also celebrated Chicago's cultural diversity. Today, the Chicago-style hot dog stands as a delicious testament to the resilience and creativity born out of necessity during the challenging times of the Depression.

Ingredients

- Vienna Beef hot dogs
- Poppy seed hot dog buns
- Yellow mustard
- Chopped white onions
- Neon-green relish
- Tomato slices
- Pickle spears
- Sport peppers
- Celery salt

Instructions

1. Grill Vienna Beef hot dogs.
2. Steam poppy seed buns.
3. Place hot dogs in buns.
4. Add yellow mustard, chopped onions, neon-green relish, tomato slices, a pickle spear, sport peppers, and a dash of celery salt.
5. Serve immediately.

Variation
The Sonoran Dog:

Wrap Chicago-style hot dog in cooked bacon. Top with pinto beans, diced tomatoes, onions, mayo, mustard, jalapeños. Serve in poppy seed bun.

The Depression Era (1930s)

Sawmill Gravy on Biscuits

Sawmill gravy on biscuits, a beloved Southern comfort dish, traces its origins to humble beginnings. Emerging during times of scarcity, particularly the Great Depression, sawmill gravy became a staple in lumber camps and rural households. The name "sawmill" alludes to its simplicity and affordability, making it accessible to those with limited resources. The gravy typically consists of pan drippings, flour, milk, salt, and pepper—basic ingredients that were readily available. Often served over freshly baked biscuits, this dish epitomizes the ingenuity born out of necessity. Families found comfort and sustenance in sawmill gravy, turning meager ingredients into a flavorful and filling meal. Today, it stands as a testament to the resourcefulness of Southern cuisine, preserving a slice of history in each velvety-smooth, creamy bite atop a warm, flaky biscuit.

Ingredients

- 1/4 cup pan drippings (bacon fat or sausage grease)
- 1/4 cup all-purpose flour
- 2 cups whole milk
- Salt and pepper to taste
- Freshly baked biscuits

Instructions

1. Heat 1/4 cup bacon fat.

2. Whisk in 1/4 cup flour for a roux.

3. Gradually add 2 cups milk, whisk until thickened.

4. Season with salt and pepper.

5. Optional: add cooked sausage or bacon.

6. Split open biscuits.

7. Ladle gravy over biscuits.

8. Serve immediately.

The Depression Era (1930s)

Corned Beef

During the Great Depression, corned beef played a crucial role as an economical and versatile protein source. Homemade corned beef, crafted by brining brisket with salt and spices, allowed families to preserve and flavor meat, extending its utility. Canned corned beef, with its convenience and extended shelf life, became a pantry staple, offering readily available sustenance during lean times. Both forms of corned beef, whether homemade or canned, were embraced for their affordability and ability to transform simple dishes. From homemade stews to canned corned beef hash, this hearty meat became a symbol of resourcefulness, providing nourishment and flavor to families navigating the challenges of economic hardship during the Depression.

Ingredients

- 1 whole beef brisket (approximately 5-6 pounds)
- Brine (below)
- 2 onions, quartered
- 4 carrots, peeled and cut into chunks
- 4 potatoes, peeled and halved
- 1 head of cabbage, cut into wedges
- Whole grain mustard for serving

For the Brine:
- 3 cups water
- 1 cup kosher salt
- 1/2 cup brown sugar
- 2 bottles of dark beer
- 1/4 cup yellow mustard
- 3 cloves garlic, minced
- 2 tablespoons pickling spice
- 1 teaspoon pink curing salt (optional)
- 1 cinnamon stick
- 1 bay leaf

Instructions

1. Brine brisket in beer-mustard mix for 5 days.

2. Rinse brisket, place in a pot with onions, cover with water.

3. Simmer on stovetop, for 20 minutes per pound- then bake at 300°F for 3 hrs to deepen flavours.

4. Add carrots, potatoes, cabbage for last 45-60 mins.

5. Slice brisket against the grain.

6. Serve with veggies and whole grain mustard.

The Depression Era (1930s)

Deviled Ham

Deviled ham, a popular canned meat product, gained prominence during the Great Depression as an affordable and convenient protein source. Typically made from ground, seasoned ham, it became a staple in households facing economic challenges. Deviled ham was prized for its versatility, offering a quick and flavorful solution to meal preparation. Families used it as a spread for sandwiches or crackers, enhancing its taste with various seasonings. The accessibility and long shelf life of canned deviled ham made it a practical choice for creating satisfying meals during times of scarcity. Its popularity endured beyond the Depression era, and to this day, deviled ham remains a nostalgic and convenient addition to many households.

Ingredients

- 2 cups cooked ham, diced
- 2 tablespoons Dijon mustard
- 2 tablespoons mayonnaise
- 1 tablespoon sweet pickle relish
- 1 teaspoon Worcestershire sauce
- 1/2 teaspoon smoked paprika
- 1/4 teaspoon cayenne pepper (adjust to taste)
- Salt and black pepper to taste
- Optional: a dash of hot sauce for extra heat

Instructions

1. In a food processor, blend 2 cups diced cooked ham.

2. Add 2 tbsp Dijon mustard, 2 tbsp mayonnaise, 1 tbsp sweet pickle relish, 1 tsp Worcestershire sauce, 1/2 tsp smoked paprika, 1/4 tsp cayenne, salt, and pepper.

3. Optionally, add hot sauce.

4. Adjust seasoning.

5. Chill for 1-2 hours.

6. Spread on crackers or bread.

7. Enjoy! Homemade deviled ham offers a flavorful and customizable twist on the classic canned version.

The Depression Era (1930s)

Vinegar Pie

Vinegar pie, a frugal yet surprisingly delicious dessert, has roots deeply embedded in American culinary history, particularly during times of scarcity like the Great Depression. Born out of necessity, this ingenious pie relies on simple ingredients like vinegar, sugar, butter, and eggs to create a tangy, custard-like filling. Its popularity surged during times when traditional pie ingredients were scarce, offering a budget-friendly alternative. The acidity of vinegar not only imparted a distinctive flavor but also served as a preservative. Families cherished this humble pie for its affordability and the ability to transform basic pantry staples into a comforting treat. While its prevalence has waned, vinegar pie remains a testament to the resourcefulness and creativity of cooks navigating challenging periods in American culinary heritage.

Ingredients

- 1 9-inch pie crust (store-bought or homemade)
- 1 cup granulated sugar
- 2 tablespoons all-purpose flour
- 3 large eggs
- 1/2 cup unsalted butter, melted
- 1 tablespoon apple cider vinegar
- 1 teaspoon vanilla extract
- Pinch of salt

Instructions

1. Mix sugar and flour.

2. Add beaten eggs, melted butter, vinegar, vanilla, and salt.

3. Pour into a pie crust.

4. Bake at 350°F for 30-35 mins.

5. Cool and slice.

The Depression Era (1930s)

Water Pie

Water pie, a testament to the creativity during the Great Depression, emerged when traditional baking ingredients were scarce. With flour, sugar, and fats in short supply, inventive cooks turned to water as the main component. The recipe typically consisted of a pie shell filled with water, sugar, and flavorings such as vanilla or spices. Though minimalist, water pie aimed to provide a semblance of sweetness and comfort during difficult times. Its simplicity reflected the resilience of families navigating economic challenges, showcasing the ability to transform basic ingredients into a treat. While water pie's popularity waned post-Depression, it remains a poignant reminder of resourcefulness and the capacity to find solace in the most humble offerings during times of adversity.

Ingredients

- 1 9-inch pie crust (store-bought or homemade)
- 2 cups bottled still water
- 1 cup granulated sugar
- 3 tablespoons all-purpose flour
- 1/4 teaspoon salt
- 1 teaspoon vanilla extract
- Ground cinnamon (optional, for garnish)

Instructions

1. Mix 2 cups water, 1 cup sugar, 3 tbsp flour, 1/4 tsp salt, and 1 tsp vanilla.

2. Pour into a 9-inch pie crust.

3. Bake at 425°F for 10 mins, then reduce to 350°F for 20-25 mins until golden.

4. Cool completely before slicing.

The Depression Era (1930s)

Tuna and Ham Casserole

The Depression-era Tuna and Ham Casserole symbolizes resourcefulness, offering a nourishing and economical meal during challenging times. With pantry staples like canned tuna, pasta, and condensed soup, families transformed humble ingredients into a hearty dish, now enhanced with the savory addition of ham. The casserole's simplicity aligns with the era's constraints, emphasizing affordability and efficiency. Tuna, a budget-friendly protein, and ham, a flavorful addition, pair seamlessly with accessible ingredients, creating a comforting and satisfying meal. Baked to perfection, the casserole not only stretched meager resources but also provided a sense of culinary warmth. This Depression-era classic, now elevated with ham, endures as a symbol of ingenuity, showcasing the ability to craft flavorful and filling dishes even amidst economic hardship.

Ingredients

- Canned tuna
- Egg noodles
- Cream of mushroom soup
- Peas
- Cheddar cheese
- Bread crumbs
- Cooked ham, diced

Super Easy Homemade Cream of Mushroom Soup:

Sauté 1lb mushrooms, onion, garlic in 3 tbsp butter. Stir in 3 tbsp flour, pour 4 cups broth, simmer 10 mins. Blend, season, add 1 cup cream, simmer 5 mins. Garnish. Serve hot, savoring the delightful creaminess of this homemade mushroom soup!

Instructions

1. Cook noodles.

2. Mix cooked noodles with tuna, soup, peas, and diced ham.

3. Top the mixture with cheese and breadcrumbs.

4. Bake the casserole at 350°F (175°C) for approximately 25-30 minutes or until it becomes bubbly and the top is golden brown. Keep an eye on it to ensure it reaches the desired level of doneness.

The Depression Era (1930s)

Campfire Canned Oyster Casserole

During the Depression, canned fish emerged as a vital pantry staple, offering an affordable and versatile source of protein. Families turned to canned goods, including tuna and smoked oysters, for their longevity and budget-friendly nature. This inspired the creation of the Campfire Canned Oyster Casserole, a nod to the ingenuity born out of scarcity. The slow-cooked dish transforms humble canned oysters, a Depression-era favorite, into a flavorful and comforting meal. The addition of liquid smoke pays homage to the campfire spirit, replicating the smoky essence of outdoor cooking. This recipe encapsulates the resourcefulness of Depression-era cooks, who transformed everyday pantry items into nourishing dishes that provided both sustenance and a sense of warmth during challenging times.

Ingredients

- 2 cans (8 oz each) smoked oysters, drained
- 1 cup crushed saltine crackers
- 1/2 cup unsalted butter, melted
- 1 cup shredded cheddar cheese
- 1/2 cup sour cream
- 1/4 cup mayonnaise
- 2 tablespoons chopped fresh parsley
- 1 teaspoon Worcestershire sauce
- 1 teaspoon liquid smoke
- Salt and pepper to taste
- Lemon wedges for serving

Instructions

1. Mix crushed crackers with melted butter for the crust.

2. Layer drained smoked oysters.

3. In a bowl, combine cheddar cheese, sour cream, mayo, parsley, Worcestershire sauce, liquid smoke, salt, and pepper.

4. Spread the mixture over the oysters.

5. Bake at 275°F for 45-50 mins.

6. Cool and serve with lemon wedges.

World War II Years (1940s)

Chicken and Sausage Étouffée

In the 1940s, Chicken and Sausage Étouffée became a significant culinary staple in the U.S., epitomizing the fusion of Cajun flavors with American comfort cuisine. This hearty dish gained prominence during wartime when creativity in the kitchen was essential due to rationing. Its one-pot simplicity and the ability to stretch ingredients made it a practical and delicious choice for American households. The rich flavors of smoked sausage, chicken, and a robust blend of spices provided both nourishment and a comforting taste of home. Amidst the challenges of the era, Chicken and Sausage Étouffée symbolized resourcefulness, culinary ingenuity, and the ability to create soul-satisfying meals, solidifying its place as a cherished dish that resonates with the resilience and spirit of the 1940s American kitchen.

Ingredients

- 1/2 cup vegetable oil
- 1/2 cup all-purpose flour
- 1 large onion, finely chopped
- 1 bell pepper, finely chopped
- 2 celery stalks, finely chopped
- 3 cloves garlic, minced
- 1 pound boneless, skinless chicken thighs, cut into bite-sized pieces
- 1/2 pound smoked sausage, sliced
- 1 teaspoon paprika
- 1 teaspoon dried thyme
- 1 teaspoon dried oregano
- 1/2 teaspoon cayenne pepper (adjust to taste)
- 2 bay leaves
- Salt and black pepper to taste
- 3 cups chicken broth
- 1 can (14 ounces) diced tomatoes
- 1/4 cup chopped fresh parsley
- 4 green onions, chopped
- Cooked rice for serving

Instructions

1. Make a roux by combining 1/2 cup oil and flour until dark.

2. Sauté onion, bell pepper, celery, and garlic in the roux until softened.

3. Add chicken and sausage, cooking until chicken is browned.

4. Season with paprika, thyme, oregano, cayenne, bay leaves, salt, and pepper.

5. Pour in 3 cups chicken broth, add diced tomatoes, and simmer for 30-40 minutes.

6. Stir in parsley and green onions.

7. Adjust seasoning if needed.

8. Serve over cooked rice. Enjoy!

World War II Years (1940s)

Cabbage Soup with Okra and Black-Eyed Peas

In the 1940s, cabbage soup gained popularity as a nutritious and economical dish amidst the constraints of wartime rationing. With ingredients like cabbage, potatoes, carrots, and broth, the soup was a testament to ingenuity in utilizing readily available items. Families embraced this hearty and filling option, adapting the recipe to suit rationed supplies while maximizing flavor. The simplicity of cabbage soup aligned with the era's emphasis on stretching ingredients to feed the family. This period marked a culinary journey where frugality and creativity converged, giving rise to comforting dishes like cabbage soup that not only sustained people through scarcity but also left an enduring mark on the culinary landscape, showcasing the resilience and resourcefulness of home cooks during challenging times.

Ingredients

- 2 cans (8 oz each) smoked
- 1 medium head of cabbage, shredded
- 3 large potatoes, diced
- 2 carrots, sliced
- 1 onion, finely chopped
- 2 cloves garlic, minced
- 1 cup cooked black-eyed peas (canned or pre-cooked)
- 1 cup sliced okra (fresh or frozen)
- 8 cups beef or vegetable broth
- 1 can (14 oz) diced tomatoes
- 2 tablespoons tomato paste
- 1 bay leaf
- 1 teaspoon dried thyme
- Salt and pepper to taste
- 2 tablespoons olive oil

Instructions

1. Sauté onions and garlic.

2. Add potatoes, carrots, okra, and black-eyed peas; cook.

3. Stir in shredded cabbage.

4. Pour broth, add tomatoes, tomato paste, bay leaf, thyme, salt, and pepper.

5. Simmer for 30-40 mins.

6. Adjust seasoning.

7. Serve hot, with crusty bread if desired.

World War II Years (1940s)

Mennonite Delicate White Cake

The 1940s witnessed the continuation of Mennonite culinary traditions, including the iconic Delicate White Cake. Rooted in simplicity and wholesome ingredients, Mennonite recipes often showcased resourcefulness and a commitment to nurturing family and community bonds. The Delicate White Cake, characterized by its tender crumb and subtle sweetness, encapsulated the essence of Mennonite baking during this era. Home bakers relied on basic pantry staples like flour, sugar, eggs, and dairy, crafting delicate cakes that served as centerpieces for various celebrations. The 1940s Mennonite kitchen reflected a balance between tradition and adaptation, as these communities maintained their culinary heritage while adapting to the challenges and changes brought about by wartime rationing and economic constraints. The Delicate White Cake became a symbol of resilience, preserving Mennonite culinary customs in a world marked by uncertainty and change.

Ingredients

- 1 cup unsalted butter, softened
- 2 cups granulated sugar
- 4 large eggs
- 3 cups cake flour
- 1 tablespoon baking powder
- 1/2 teaspoon salt
- 1 cup whole milk
- 1 teaspoon vanilla extract
- 1/2 teaspoon almond extract (optional)

Instructions

1. Cream butter and sugar.
2. Add eggs.
3. Sift flour, baking powder, and salt.
4. Alternately add dry ingredients and milk.
5. Stir in vanilla and almond extract.
6. Bake in two pans at 350°F for 25-30 mins.
7. Cool, then frost.

World War II Years (1940s)

Philly Cheesesteak

In the 1930s, the iconic Philly Cheesesteak originated when Pat Olivieri, a South Philadelphia hot dog vendor, ventured beyond hot dogs, experimenting with thinly sliced beef on an Italian roll. By the 1940s, the cheesesteak took a historic turn when a manager at Pat's King of Steaks introduced melted provolone to the sandwich. This savory addition resonated with patrons, marking a pivotal moment in the sandwich's evolution. The melding of succulent ribeye, grilled to perfection, and gooey cheese became the hallmark of the authentic Philly Cheesesteak we relish today. This 1940s innovation transformed a modest hot dog stand creation into a culinary legend, emblematic of Philadelphia's rich food culture and celebrated worldwide for its delectable combination of flavors and textures.

Ingredients

- 1.5 pounds ribeye steak, partially frozen for easier slicing
- 4 Italian rolls
- 1 large onion, thinly sliced
- 1 large bell pepper, thinly sliced
- 8 slices provolone cheese
- Salt and pepper to taste
- Olive oil for cooking
- Optional: hot cherry peppers for extra kick

Instructions

1. Partially freeze 1.5 lbs ribeye for 45-90 mins.

2. Slice thinly. The key secret method : slicing the partially frozen ribeye ensures thin, tender perfection for your authentic Philly Cheesesteak.

3. Sauté onions and bell peppers.

4. Cook ribeye in a hot skillet until browned.

5. Melt provolone over beef.

6. Add sautéed veggies.

7. Toast Italian rolls.

8. Assemble, optionally adding hot cherry peppers.

World War II Years (1940s)

Grandma's Potato Salad

In the 1940s, potato salad in the U.S. thrived despite wartime rationing. Traditional recipes, rooted in boiled potatoes, mayonnaise, and mustard, faced creative adaptations due to ingredient shortages. Regional influences shaped variations, with Southern versions embracing mustard, pickles, and eggs, while Northern styles favored creamier textures with mayonnaise. German and Eastern European immigrants contributed recipes featuring vinegar and bacon. The decade witnessed the advent of convenience foods, introducing store-bought mayonnaise and diversifying ingredient choices. Post-war, as rationing eased, potato salad evolved, with some recipes adopting tangy flavors using sour cream or yogurt. Today, the legacy of 1940s potato salad endures, embodying regional diversity and culinary ingenuity in the classic American repertoire.

Ingredients

- 2 lbs potatoes, boiled and diced
- 1/2 cup mayonnaise
- 1/4 cup Dijon mustard
- 1/4 cup chopped pickles
- 2 tablespoons pickle juice
- 1/8 cup chopped chives of shallots
- Salt and pepper to taste
- Chopped fresh dill for garnish

Instructions

1. Combine boiled potatoes, mayo, mustard, pickles, pickle juice, and chives or shallots.

2. Season to taste.

3. Garnish with fresh dill.

4. Chill before serving.

World War II Years (1940s)

Key Lime Pie

The culinary history of Key Lime Pie in the 1940s reflects its deep roots in Florida's cuisine. While the exact origin of the pie remains debated, its popularity surged during this era, coinciding with improved accessibility to condensed milk.

The traditional Key Lime Pie recipe typically involves a graham cracker crust, a filling made with Key lime juice, sweetened condensed milk, and egg yolks, topped with meringue or whipped cream. The use of Key limes, native to the Florida Keys, adds a distinctive tartness.

In the 1940s, as condensed milk became more prevalent, Key Lime Pie gained widespread recognition. The pie's simplicity, vibrant flavor, and association with Florida's tropical landscape contributed to its popularity. Though variations existed, the 1940s marked a pivotal period for Key Lime Pie, solidifying its place as a beloved dessert in American culinary history.

Ingredients

For the Crust:
- 1 1/2 cups graham cracker crumbs
- 1/3 cup melted butter
- 1/4 cup granulated sugar

For the Filling:
- 1 can (14 ounces) sweetened condensed milk
- 4 large egg yolks
- 1/2 cup Key lime juice (freshly squeezed if possible)

For the Topping:
- 1 cup whipped cream or meringue (optional)

Instructions

1. Mix graham cracker crumbs, melted butter, sugar. Press into a 9-inch pie dish. Bake at 350°F for 8-10 mins until lightly golden. Cool before filling.

2. Whisk condensed milk, egg yolks, Key lime juice for the filling.

3. Pour the filling into the crust and bake at 350°F (175°C) for approximately 15 minutes or until the center is set. Keep an eye on it, as baking times may vary slightly.

4. Allow the pie to cool to room temperature before refrigerating for at least 2 hours or until fully chilled.

5. Cool and refrigerate.

6. Top with whipped cream.

7. Garnish with lime zest.

World War II Years (1940s)

Chicken-fried Steak

The history of Chicken-fried Steak can be traced back to the Texas Hill Country in the early 20th century, and its popularity continued to grow in the 1940s. This comfort food is associated with Southern and Southwestern American cuisines.

In the 1940s, during and after World War II, Chicken-fried Steak became a staple in diners and home kitchens. The dish was economical and utilized less expensive cuts of meat, typically cube steak, which was tenderized and coated in flour, much like fried chicken. It was then pan-fried to a golden brown and served with a creamy white gravy.

The dish resonated with the times, offering a hearty and satisfying meal that was both economical and flavorful. Chicken-fried Steak's enduring popularity reflects its status as a classic American comfort food, cherished for its simplicity and down-home appeal.

Ingredients

For the Steak:
- 4 cube steaks
- Salt and pepper to taste
- 1 cup all-purpose flour
- 2 large eggs
- 1/2 cup buttermilk
- Lard or Peanut Oil for frying

For the Gravy:
- 1/4 cup pan drippings
- 1/4 cup all-purpose flour
- 2 cups whole milk
- Salt and pepper to taste

Instructions

1. Season cube steaks.

2. Dredge in flour, dip in an egg-buttermilk mixture, coat again in flour.

3. Fry in hot oil until golden brown. Drain on paper towels.

4. Reserve 1/4 cup pan drippings.

5. Whisk in 1/4 cup flour, cook until golden.

6. Gradually whisk in milk, cook until thickened.

7. Season with salt and pepper, and, pour creamy gravy over fried steaks.

9. Serve with mashed potatoes.

World War II Years (1940s)

Clam Linguine

In the 1940s, Clam Linguine epitomized the fusion of Italian and American culinary influences. As Italian immigrants left an indelible mark on American gastronomy, seafood dishes gained prominence. Clam Linguine, featuring linguine pasta, fresh clams, garlic, white wine, olive oil, and parsley, became a symbol of this culinary exchange. The era's emphasis on locally available ingredients, driven by World War II rationing, further elevated the dish's appeal. The simplicity and elegance of Clam Linguine mirrored the innovative spirit of 1940s kitchens, where resourcefulness and a love for flavorful combinations converged. This period laid the foundation for the enduring popularity of Clam Linguine as a cherished Italian-American classic, capturing the essence of both cultures in a single, delectable dish.

Ingredients

- 12 ounces linguine pasta
- 2 tablespoons olive oil
- 4 cloves garlic, minced
- 1/2 teaspoon red pepper flakes (optional for a bit of heat)
- 1 cup dry white wine
- 2 dozen littleneck clams, scrubbed
- Salt and black pepper to taste
- Fresh parsley, chopped, for garnish
- Grated Parmesan cheese (optional)

Instructions

1. Cook linguine until *al dente*.

2. Sauté minced garlic in olive oil, add red pepper flakes if desired.

3. Pour white wine into the skillet, add cleaned clams, cover, and simmer until opened.

4. Season with salt and pepper.

5. Toss cooked linguine into the skillet, ensuring it's well-coated.

6. Garnish with fresh parsley, sprinkle with Parmesan if desired.

7. Serve warm, discarding any unopened clams.

World War II Years (1940s)

Diner Fried Bologna Sandwich, *or*
Gourmet Grilled Mortadella and Bologna Duo with Emmental and Sharp Cheddar

In the 1940s, diners became quintessential Americana, embodying the post-war spirit and evolving culinary trends. Diners were cherished for their nostalgic charm, offering affordable comfort food in a communal atmosphere. Our fictional, imagined Diner Fried Bologna Sandwich pays homage to this era, reminiscent of the simple yet hearty fare served in diners. Fried bologna sandwiches were a staple, reflecting the resourcefulness of the time. The sandwich, featuring seared bologna slices on griddled bread, captures the essence of diner classics. It symbolizes the ingenuity and affordability of 1940s diners, where unpretentious dishes gained a cherished place in culinary history, creating a timeless and comforting experience for generations. I am poshing this one up a bit.

Ingredients

- 8 slices mortadella
- 8 slices thick-cut bologna
- 4 slices Emmental cheese
- 4 slices sharp cheddar cheese
- 1 Spanish onion, thinly sliced and caramelized
- 1/4 cup Dijon mustard
- 1/4 cup mayonnaise
- 8 slices brioche bread
- Butter for grilling
- Salt and pepper to taste
- Fresh arugula for garnish

Instructions

1. Grill mortadella and bologna 1-2 minutes per side for a seared and crispy texture.

2. Make aioli with Dijon mustard and mayonnaise.

3. Layer brioche with Emmental, sharp cheddar, grilled mortadella, bologna, and caramelized onions.

4. Top with aioli and another slice of brioche.

5. Grill until golden and cheese melts.

6. Garnish with arugula.

World War II Years (1940s)

Cheese & Tomato Mashed Potato Pie

During the 1940s, the Cheese & Tomato Mashed Potato Pie emerged as a comforting and resourceful dish, reflecting the challenges of World War II rationing. With ingredients in short supply, cooks creatively adapted recipes to make satisfying meals. Mashed potatoes served as a cost-effective and versatile base, while cheese and tomatoes added flavor and nutrients. The pie's simplicity and reliance on pantry staples made it a popular choice for families on a budget. As wartime restrictions influenced culinary innovation, this dish exemplified the resilience of home cooks, turning basic ingredients into a flavorful, filling meal. The Cheese & Tomato Mashed Potato Pie from the 1940s remains a testament to the era's ingenuity and adaptability in the face of adversity.

Ingredients

- 4 cups mashed potatoes
- 1 cup sharp cheddar cheese, shredded
- 1/2 cup Parmesan cheese, grated
- 1/2 cup Gruyère cheese, s shredded
- 2 cloves garlic, minced
- 2 tablespoons fresh thyme, finely chopped
- Salt and pepper to taste
- 2 large tomatoes, thinly sliced
- Fresh basil for garnish

Instructions

1. Mix garlic and thyme into 4 cups mashed potatoes.

2. Layer half of the mashed potatoes in a greased dish.

3. Add cheddar, Parmesan, and Gruyère to the layer.

4. Top with sliced tomatoes.

5. Repeat the layers with the remaining mashed potatoes, cheeses, and tomatoes.

6. Bake at 375°F for 30-35 minutes.

7. Garnish with fresh basil.

The Post-War Boom (1950s)

TV Dinner: Salisbury Steak with Mashed Potatoes and Buttered Flageolets

In the 1950s, TV dinners emerged as a transformative solution for post-war American families, revolutionizing mealtime with unparalleled convenience. Companies like Swanson introduced these pre-packaged meals, featuring compartmentalized trays that mirrored the era's fascination with television. The Salisbury steak, rooted in Dr. James Salisbury's 19th-century dietary principles centered around minced beef, evolved into a cornerstone of TV dinners by the 1950s. This seasoned ground beef patty not only represented the adaptation of culinary traditions but also embodied the quick and satisfying meal ethos that resonated with the fast-paced lifestyle of the time.

Flageolet beans, prized for their delicate flavor and creamy texture in French cuisine, transcended borders and became a versatile ingredient in diverse international dishes. These beans, with their unique taste and nutritional profile, continue to enrich meals worldwide, showcasing the enduring influence of culinary innovations from different eras.

Ingredients

For the Salisbury Steak:
- 1.5 lbs ground beef
- 2 tbsp crushed black peppercorns
- 1 tsp salt
- 1 tsp Worcestershire sauce
- 1 egg
- 2 tbsp breadcrumbs
- 2 tbsp olive oil

For the Brandy Sauce:
- 1 cup beef broth
- 1/2 cup brandy
- 2 tbsp unsalted butter
- 1 tbsp all-purpose flour
- Salt and pepper to taste

For the Mashed Potatoes:
- 4 large potatoes, peeled and diced
- 1/2 cup milk
- 4 tbsp unsalted butter
- Salt and pepper to taste

For the Flageolet Beans:
- 1 cup flageolet beans, cooked
- 2 tbsp olive oil
- 2 cloves garlic, minced
- 1 tsp fresh thyme leaves
- Salt and pepper to taste

Instructions

1. Mix Worcestershire, peppercorn, egg, and breadcrumbs into beef patties.

2. Sear the patties in olive oil.

3. For the brandy sauce, melt butter, add flour, then gradually whisk in broth and brandy. Simmer.

4. Boil and mash potatoes with milk and butter.

5. Sauté garlic in olive oil, add flageolet beans and thyme.

6. Plate the steak on mashed potatoes, spoon the sauce, and serve with flageolet beans.

The Post-War Boom (1950s)

Cuban Sandwich

The Cuban sandwich, a beloved Latin-American culinary creation, gained popularity in the 1950s, particularly in Cuban communities in Florida. A distinctive element contributing to its unique texture and flavor is the traditional use of lard in the bread-making process. Lard, a rendered pork fat, imparts a pastry-like texture and lift to the bread, setting it apart from other sandwich varieties. This technique reflects the influence of Cuban and Spanish baking traditions. By the 1950s, the Cuban sandwich had become a common and cherished street food, featuring layers of ham, roast pork, Swiss cheese, pickles, mustard, and the characteristic lard-enriched bread. Its widespread availability and delicious combination of flavors contributed to its status as a cultural icon, emblematic of the vibrant fusion of culinary influences in Cuban-American communities during this era.

Ingredients

For the Bread:
- 3 1/2 cups all-purpose flour
- 2 tsp salt
- 1 tbsp sugar
- 2 tsp active dry yeast
- 1/4 cup lard, melted
- 1 cup warm water

For the Roast Pork:
- 2 lbs pork shoulder, boneless
- 3 cloves garlic, minced
- 1 tsp cumin
- 1 tsp oregano
- Salt and pepper to taste
 1/4 cup orange juice
 1/4 cup lime juice

For Assembly:
- Yellow mustard
- Dill pickles, sliced
- Swiss cheese, sliced
- Sliced ham

Instructions

Bread:
1. Mix 3.5 cups flour, 2 tsp salt, 1 tbsp sugar, and 2 tsp yeast.
2. Add 1/4 cup melted lard and 1 cup warm water.
3. Knead, fold several times, rise, shape, and fold 2-3x more.
4. Pinch the bottom to seal the dough and let it sit for 20 minutes.
5. Bake at 375°F for layers and crunch.

Roast Pork:
Rub 2 lbs pork with garlic, cumin, oregano, salt, pepper. Marinate in 1/4 cup orange/lime juice. Roast at 325°F until internal temp of 145°F.

Assembly:
Slice, spread mustard, layer ham, roast pork, pickles, Swiss cheese. Fold, press in a panini press for meltiness and crispiness.

The Post-War Boom (1950s)

Pineapple Lime Cheese Salad

In the 1950s, the Lime Cheese Salad emerged as a peculiar culinary creation, reflective of the era's fascination with novel flavor combinations and convenient, processed foods. This quirky dish typically featured lime-flavored gelatin, cream cheese, mayonnaise, and various canned fruits like pineapple or pears. The salad, often served molded into intricate shapes, embodied the mid-century obsession with incorporating unexpected ingredients into traditional recipes. Its popularity was fueled by the convenience of canned and processed foods during a time marked by post-war optimism and the advent of time-saving kitchen innovations. The Lime Cheese Salad stands as a quirky testament to the culinary experimentation and evolving tastes that characterized the 1950s, providing a glimpse into the unique food trends of that era.

Ingredients

- Lime gelatin
- Cream cheese
- Crushed pineapple (drained)
- Shredded coconut
- Mandarin orange segments

Note: Pineapple contains an enzyme called bromelain, which can interfere with the setting of gelatin

For a successful Tropical Lime Cheese Salad, use canned pineapple, drain thoroughly, and add post-cooling to counteract bromelain interference with gelatin setting.

Instructions

1. Prepare lime gelatin as directed.

2. Mix in softened cream cheese, crushed pineapple, shredded coconut, and mandarin orange segments.

3. Chill until firm.

4. Garnish with additional coconut and serve.

The Post-War Boom (1950s)

Ham Banana Rolls

The Ham Banana Rolls, emblematic of the culinary trends prevalent in the 1950s, reflect an era marked by an adventurous spirit in the kitchen. Crafted by enveloping slices of ham around whole bananas, this creation, whether baked or broiled to achieve a crispy texture, exemplifies the innovative approach to flavor combinations. Frequently featured in mid-century cookbooks and showcased at gatherings, these rolls signify a period when culinary experimentation was embraced with zeal. The Ham Banana Rolls, despite eliciting diverse opinions, stand as a nostalgic representation of an era where modern avant-garde chefs might applaud the audacity to explore unconventional pairings, underscoring the pursuit of creating distinct and memorable dishes in the mid-20th century culinary landscape.

Ingredients

- Sliced ham
- Ripe bananas
- Honey
- Dijon mustard

Instructions

1. Lay out ham slices.

2. Place a banana at one end, roll up tightly.

3. Secure with toothpicks.

4. Mix honey and Dijon mustard for glaze.

5. Brush glaze over rollups.

6. Bake at 375°F until ham is crispy.

7. Serve warm, drizzling extra glaze if desired.

Variation
Fiesta Fusion Glaze

1. Spread cream cheese on ham, add jalapeños, roll with banana.

2. Mix 1/2 cup mango puree, 2 tbsp chopped chipotle peppers in adobo, 2 tbsp honey, and 1 tbsp lime juice. Brush over rollups before baking.

The spicy mango-chipotle glaze is intended as an additional flavor element to enhance the Fiesta Fusion variation. You would brush the ham and banana rollups with the honey Dijon mix first and then drizzle or brush the spicy mango-chipotle glaze on top before baking. The combination of both glazes contributes to a unique and flavorful taste experience, combining sweet, savory, and spicy notes. Adjust the quantities based on your taste preferences.

The Post-War Boom (1950s)

Rumaki

In the 1950s, Tiki-inspired cuisine featured the popular Rumaki, a dish of bacon-wrapped chicken livers and water chestnuts originating in the 1920s. Reflecting the exotic tastes of the era, these lavish bites captured the prosperity and indulgence of the Roaring Twenties. The fusion of chicken livers, water chestnuts, and bacon symbolized a move towards sophistication.

It's worth noting that soy sauce, a key ingredient in the marinade, wasn't widely available until the 1950s. This inclusion, alongside sherry, highlighted the era's fascination with global flavors and mirrored the growing accessibility of international ingredients. Rumaki thus stands as a symbol of the extravagant and experimental spirit of the 1920s, contributing significantly to a vibrant culinary landscape that embraced bold flavors and innovative combinations, especially within the context of the 1950s Tiki food trend.

Ingredients

- 1 pound chicken livers, trimmed and cut into bite-sized pieces
- 1 can (8 oz) water chestnuts, whole or halved
- 1 cup soy sauce
- 1 cup brown sugar
- 1/2 cup olive oil
- 1/4 cup dry sherry
- 1 teaspoon ground ginger
- Bacon slices, cut into halves
- Toothpicks

Instructions

1. Trim livers to remove excess fat and connective tissue for enhanced flavor and texture.

2. Marinate in soy sauce, brown sugar, olive oil, sherry, and ginger.

3. After 30 mins, wrap each liver and water chestnut with bacon, secure with toothpicks.

4. Bake at 400°F for 15-20 mins until bacon is crispy.

5. Remove toothpicks before serving.

The Post-War Boom (1950s)

Cheesy Beer Green Bean Casserole

The Green Bean Casserole, an iconic American dish, emerged in the 1950s as a testament to the era's culinary convenience and the rise of processed foods. Created by Dorcas Reilly for the Campbell Soup Company, the original recipe featured canned green beans, condensed cream of mushroom soup, and crispy fried onions. Introduced as an easy-to-prepare side dish, the casserole quickly gained popularity, becoming a staple on Thanksgiving tables and beyond.

Its widespread adoption was fueled by its simplicity, affordability, and the convenience of utilizing readily available canned ingredients during a time when home cooking increasingly incorporated convenience foods. The Green Bean Casserole's enduring appeal has solidified its place as a nostalgic and beloved dish, illustrating the cultural and culinary trends of the 1950s, where innovation and efficiency played a significant role in shaping American home cooking.

Ingredients

For the Condensed Cheddar Cheese Soup:
- 2 tbsp butter
- 2 tbsp all-purpose flour
- 1 cup milk
- 1 cup shredded cheddar cheese
- Salt and pepper to taste

For the Cheesy Green Bean Casserole:
- 2 cans (14 oz each) green beans, drained
- Homemade condensed cheddar cheese soup
- 1/2 cup beer (light or dark, as per preference)
- 1/2 cup sour cream
- 1/2 tsp garlic powder
- Salt and pepper to taste
- 1 1/2 cups crispy fried onions

Instructions

For 'Condensed' Cheddar Cheese Soup:
1. Melt 2 tbsp butter, add 2 tbsp flour, cook.

2. Gradually whisk in 1 cup milk.

3. Add 1 cup shredded cheddar, salt, and pepper.

4. Stir until creamy.

For Cheesy Green Bean Casserole:
1. Mix 2 cans green beans, homemade condensed cheddar cheese soup, 1/2 cup beer, 1/2 cup sour cream, garlic powder, salt, and pepper in a dish.

2. Top with 1 1/2 cups fried onions.

3. Bake at 375°F for 25 mins.

4. Serve warm.!

The Post-War Boom (1950s)

Fried Catfish

Fried catfish has deep roots in Southern cuisine, and its popularity continued to grow in the 1950s. With the post-war economic boom and increased accessibility to frozen foods, catfish farming became more prevalent. The 1950s marked a period when Southern culinary traditions gained broader recognition.

Fried catfish, often coated in cornmeal for a crispy texture, was a staple in Southern households and soul food establishments. This dish became symbolic of comfort and home-cooked goodness. The rise of interstate highways and increased mobility further contributed to the spread of Southern culinary traditions, including the beloved fried catfish. It wasn't just a meal; it became a cultural icon, reflecting the rich history and flavors of the American South.

Ingredients

- 4 catfish fillets
- 2 cups buttermilk
- 1 cup cornmeal
- 1 cup all-purpose flour
- 1 teaspoon paprika
- 1 teaspoon garlic powder
- Salt and pepper to taste
- Peanut oil for frying

Sauce Options:

Tangy Tartar Sauce:
Blend mayo, chopped capers, diced pickles, lemon juice, and a dash of Worcestershire.

Chipotle Lime Crema:
Whisk together sour cream, chipotle in adobo, lime juice, and a pinch of cumin.

Instructions

1. Marinate catfish in buttermilk for 1 hour.

2. Dredge in a mix of cornmeal, flour, paprika, garlic powder, salt, and pepper.

3. Fry until golden brown in 350°F oil.

4. Drain and serve hot.

The Post-War Boom (1950s)

Shredded BBQ Chicken & Tater Tot Casserole

Tater tots, those beloved bite-sized potato cylinders, have a humble yet fascinating history. In the 1950s, two brothers, F. Nephi Grigg and Golden Grigg, co-founders of the Ore-Ida brand, were looking for an innovative way to use the leftover potato scraps from their frozen French fry production. They decided to chop up the scraps, season them, and then press them into bite-sized cylinders. The result was the birth of tater tots in 1953.

Initially, tater tots were not an instant hit, but their popularity surged in the following decades. Their convenient size, crispy exterior, and fluffy interior made them a staple in school cafeterias and a favorite among families. Today, tater tots are a nostalgic comfort food enjoyed in various forms, from classic to gourmet, and continue to hold a special place in American culinary culture.

Ingredients

- 2 cups cooked shredded chicken
- 1 cup homemade barbecue sauce
- 1 can (15 oz) black beans, drained
- 1 cup corn kernels
- 2 cups shredded pepper jack cheese
- Homemade tater tots

When frying homemade tater tots, heat the oil to a temperature of around 350°F to 375°F (175°C to 190°C). Fry the tater tots in small batches, ensuring they are submerged in the oil but not overcrowded. Fry them for about 2-3 minutes or until they turn golden brown and crisp. Adjust the time as needed, and always monitor the temperature of the oil to maintain a consistent frying environment.

Instructions

For Tater tots:
Grate potatoes, squeeze out as much moisture as possible. Mix with flour, salt, pepper. Shape into cylinders. Fry in 350F oil until golden brown.

For Homemade BBQ sauce:
Combine 1 cup ketchup, 1/4 cup apple cider vinegar, 2 tbsp brown sugar, 1 tbsp Worcestershire sauce, and a pinch of cayenne.

For Casserole:
1. Mix shredded chicken, barbecue sauce, black beans, and corn. Spread mixture in a baking dish.
2. Top with shredded pepper jack cheese and arrange frozen tater tots.
3. Bake at 375°F for 25-30 minutes or until tater tots are crispy.

The Post-War Boom (1950s)

Spicy Jalapeño and Pepper Jack Frankfurter Soup

The culinary history of Frankfurter Cheese Soup in the 1950s reflects a time of creativity in American home kitchens. This hearty soup often featured sliced frankfurters, cheese, vegetables, and a creamy base. In the post-World War II era, convenience foods gained popularity, and canned soups became staples in many households. Frankfurter Cheese Soup, with its simplicity and use of readily available ingredients, emerged as a comforting and economical dish. It embodied the era's focus on convenience, reflecting the evolving tastes and culinary trends of the 1950s. The soup not only provided a warm and filling meal but also showcased the ingenuity of homemakers adapting to a changing food landscape during this post-war period.

Ingredients

- 1 cup sliced frankfurters
- 1 cup diced bell peppers (assorted colors)
- 2 jalapeños, finely chopped
- 1 onion, finely diced
- 2 cloves garlic, minced
- 4 cups chicken broth
- 1 cup diced potatoes
- 1 teaspoon cayenne pepper
- 1 teaspoon paprika
- Salt and black pepper to taste
- 1 cup shredded Pepper Jack cheese
- 1/2 cup heavy cream
- Fresh cilantro for garnish

Instructions

1. Sauté frankfurters, onions, garlic, bell peppers, and jalapeños.

2. Add chicken broth, diced potatoes, cayenne, paprika, salt, and pepper.

3. Simmer until potatoes are tender.

4. Stir in shredded Pepper Jack cheese.

5. Add heavy cream for creaminess.

6. Garnish with cilantro.

1957 Hawaiian Pizza

The Hawaiian pizza, featuring pineapple, papaya, and chopped green pepper but without ham or bacon, made its debut in Portland, Oregon, in 1957. Created by Canadian Sam Panopoulos, who operated a pizzeria with his brothers, the unconventional combination was a departure from traditional pizza toppings. Inspired by the sweet and savory flavors, Panopoulos coined the term "Hawaiian" to evoke a sense of tropical paradise. Despite initial skepticism, the pizza gained popularity for its unique taste. The 1950s context, marked by culinary experimentation and the rise of convenient frozen foods, allowed for the Hawaiian pizza to carve its niche in the pizza landscape, evolving into a polarizing yet enduring favorite around the world.

Italian 00 flour offers a fine, soft texture and high gluten for elasticity. Semolina adds a gritty texture, golden color, and nutty flavor, creating a chewy, light, and flavorful pizza crust.

Ingredients

- Pizza dough (homemade or store-bought)
- 1 cup tomato sauce
- 2 cups mozzarella cheese, shredded
- 1 cup pineapple chunks, drained
- 1/2 cup papaya slices
- 1/2 cup green pepper, chopped

For Homemade Pizza Dough:
- 2 1/4 teaspoons (1 packet) active dry yeast
- 1 teaspoon sugar
- 3/4 cup warm water (110°F/43°C)
- 2 cups Italian 00 flour
- 1/4 cup semolina flour
- 1 teaspoon salt
- 1 tablespoon olive oil

Instructions

For the Dough:
1. Mix Italian 00 flour, semolina, yeast, sugar, salt, olive oil, and water.

2. Knead for 10 mins.

3. Let the dough rise for 1-2 hours.

For the Pizza:
1. Roll out pizza dough.

2. Spread tomato sauce.

3. Sprinkle mozzarella.

4. Add pineapple, papaya, and green pepper.

5. Bake in a preheated oven at 450°F (230°C) for 12-15 minutes or until crust is golden and cheese is melted.

The Post-War Boom (1950s)

Vegas Shrimp Cocktail

The Vegas Shrimp Cocktail, iconic in the 1950s, emerged as a culinary delight in the vibrant atmosphere of Las Vegas. Originating from the city's bustling casino scene, the dish featured succulent shrimp served with a zesty cocktail sauce, capturing the essence of the era's glamorous and indulgent dining experiences. With the Rat Pack and celebrities frequenting Las Vegas, the shrimp cocktail became a symbol of sophistication and entertainment. The juxtaposition of the desert locale with this seafood classic showcased the city's ability to offer the unexpected. As visitors flocked to the famous Strip, the Vegas Shrimp Cocktail epitomized the culinary innovation and flair that defined Las Vegas in the 1950s. Keeping in the spirit of the times, we are going *lux* on this one with a Alaskan King Crab and Jumbo Shrimp Tower.

Ingredients

- 1 lb Alaskan King Crab legs, cooked and chilled
- 1 lb Jumbo Shrimp, peeled, deveined, and poached

Cocktail Sauce:
- 1 cup ketchup
- 1/4 cup prepared horseradish
- 2 tablespoons fresh lemon juice
- 1 tablespoon Worcestershire sauce
- Salt and pepper to taste
- Lemon wedges for garnish
- Fresh parsley for garnish
- Optional: Edible flowers for decoration

Instructions

1. Layer chilled Alaskan King Crab and poached Jumbo Shrimp alternately in a serving glass.

2. Drizzle with a zesty cocktail sauce made with ketchup, horseradish, lemon juice, and Worcestershire.

3. Garnish with lemon wedges, fresh parsley, and optional edible flowers.

4. Serve immediately for a luxurious experience of the Alaskan King Crab and Jumbo Shrimp Tower..

The Gourmet Revolution (1960s)

Julia Child Inspired:
Simple Coq au Vin Blanc with Tarragon Mash

Julia Child, a towering figure in the emerging celebrity gourmet movement of the 1960s, revolutionized American kitchens through her passion for French cuisine. With the publication of "Mastering the Art of French Cooking" in 1961 and her iconic television series "The French Chef," she demystified complex dishes, making gourmet cooking accessible. "Coq au Vin Blanc with Tarragon Mash" exemplifies Child's impact, embodying the era's sophisticated yet approachable culinary ethos. The dish features tender chicken simmered in white wine, showcasing the French technique of braising. Paired with tarragon-infused mashed potatoes, this recipe encapsulates Child's dedication to introducing Americans to the joy of cooking and the elegance of French gastronomy, marking a pivotal moment in the democratization of gourmet cuisine during the celebrity chef movement of the 1960s.

Ingredients

- 4 chicken thighs
- 1 cup white wine
- 1 onion, chopped
- 2 cloves garlic, minced
- 1 cup chicken broth
- 2 tablespoons butter
- Salt and pepper to taste

Tarragon Mash:
- 4 large potatoes, peeled and diced
- 1/4 cup fresh tarragon, chopped
- 1/2 cup milk
- Salt and butter to taste

To sear chicken in butter, heat a pan over medium-high. Add butter, let it melt and foam. Place seasoned chicken in the pan, cook until golden brown on each side, ensuring a flavorful crust. Adjust heat to prevent burning.

Instructions

1. Season chicken and sear it in butter.

2. Add onions, garlic, white wine, and chicken broth.

3. Simmer until the chicken is cooked.

4. Boil potatoes and mash them with milk, butter, salt, and tarragon.

5. Plate the chicken over the tarragon mash.

6. Spoon the sauce over the chicken.

7. Garnish with extra tarragon.

The Gourmet Revolution (1960s)

Julia Child Inspired:
Sole Meunière with Lemon-Caper Brown Butter

Julia Child's influence on the 1960s celebrity chef culture shines through her iconic recipe, Sole Meunière with Lemon-Caper Brown Butter. This dish, with its delicate sole fillets, exemplifies the era's emphasis on classical French techniques and elevated dining. As Child demystified French cuisine in her seminal work, "Mastering the Art of French Cooking," Sole Meunière became a symbol of accessible gourmet cooking. The meticulous preparation, from dredging the fish in flour to the final touch of caper-infused brown butter, showcased the precision and artistry of French culinary traditions. Through her television series, "The French Chef," Child inspired a generation to embrace the elegance of fine dining, cementing her role in the celebrity chef movement and forever altering America's culinary landscape. Sole Meunière stands as a timeless testament to her enduring legacy and the power of her culinary teachings.

Ingredients

- 4 sole fillets
- Salt and pepper to taste
- 1/2 cup all-purpose flour
- 4 tablespoons unsalted butter
- Juice of 1 lemon
- 2 tablespoons capers, drained
- Fresh parsley for garnish

Instructions

1. Season the sole and dredge it in flour.

2. Sear the sole in butter until golden brown on both sides.

3. Remove the sole from the pan after it's cooked through.

4. In the same pan, melt more butter, add lemon juice, and capers. Cook briefly.

6. Pour the sauce over the sole.

7. Garnish with parsley.

The Gourmet Revolution (1960s)

James Beard Inspired:
Pacific Northwest Salmon Chowder

In the 1960s, James Beard, a culinary luminary, played a pivotal role in shaping American gastronomy. Renowned for his passion for local, seasonal ingredients, Beard's influence during this era extended beyond his acclaimed cookbooks to his advocacy for American cuisine's diversity. Our "James Beard Inspired Pacific Northwest Salmon Chowder" pays homage to his legacy. Bursting with flavors characteristic of the Pacific Northwest, this chowder showcases fresh salmon, potatoes, and vegetables in a rich, creamy broth. Echoing Beard's commitment to regional ingredients, the dish embodies the essence of the vibrant food culture he championed. Through this inspired recipe, we celebrate Beard's enduring impact on American cooking, especially during the dynamic culinary landscape of the 1960s.

Ingredients

- 1 lb fresh salmon, diced
- 2 tablespoons butter
- 1 onion, diced
- 2 carrots, diced
- 2 celery stalks, chopped
- 3 potatoes, peeled and cubed
- 4 cups fish or vegetable broth
- 1 cup whole milk
- 1 cup heavy cream
- 2 tablespoons all-purpose flour
- Salt and pepper to taste
- Fresh dill for garnish

Instructions

1. Sauté onions, carrots, and celery in butter.

2. Add potatoes and fish or vegetable broth, simmer until tender.

3. In a separate pan, lightly cook diced salmon.

4. Mix flour into the pot.

5. Pour in milk and heavy cream, stir until thickened.

6. Gently fold in the cooked salmon.

7. Season with salt and pepper.

8. Ladle into bowls.

9. Garnish with fresh dill and serve warm.

The Gourmet Revolution (1960s)

James Beard Inspired:
Oregon Hazelnut-Crusted Chicken

Exemplifying James Beard's dedication to regional flavors, our "James Beard Inspired Oregon Hazelnut-Crusted Chicken" pays homage to the Pacific Northwest's culinary treasures. Beard, a champion of local ingredients, emphasized the importance of regionality in American cuisine. This dish captures the essence of Oregon's renowned hazelnuts, coating tender chicken with a flavorful hazelnut crust. The Pacific Northwest's unique terroir is celebrated in each bite, showcasing the marriage of hazelnuts and succulent chicken. By honoring regional distinctions, this recipe echoes Beard's commitment to fostering an appreciation for local bounty, making it not just a delightful culinary experience but a tribute to the vibrant and diverse flavors that define the culinary landscape of the Pacific Northwest and Beard's enduring culinary philosophy.

Ingredients

- 4 boneless, skinless chicken breasts
- 1 cup Oregon hazelnuts, finely chopped
- 1/2 cup breadcrumbs
- Salt and pepper to taste
- 2 eggs, beaten
- 2 tablespoons olive oil

Instructions

1. After coating the chicken in beaten eggs and the hazelnut mixture, heat olive oil in an oven-safe skillet over medium-high heat.
2. Sear the hazelnut-crusted chicken on both sides until it develops a beautiful golden-brown crust.
3. Once adequately seared, transfer the skillet with the chicken to a preheated oven at 375°F (190°C) to finish baking.
4. This dual cooking method—searing on the stovetop and finishing in the oven—ensures a crispy exterior while maintaining the chicken's juiciness.
5. Bake for approximately 20 minutes or until the internal temperature reaches 165°F (74°C).

The Gourmet Revolution (1960s)

Craig Claiborne Inspired:
Manhattan Clam Chow Mein

In the culinary landscape of the 1960s, Craig Claiborne emerged as a trailblazing figure, leaving an indelible mark on American gastronomy. As The New York Times food editor, Claiborne influenced culinary journalism, introducing readers to diverse cuisines. Our "Craig Claiborne Inspired Manhattan Clam Chow Mein" pays tribute to his passion for exploring unique flavors. This dish mirrors Claiborne's cosmopolitan palate, blending Eastern and Western influences seamlessly. A medley of tender clams, crisp vegetables, and noodles bathed in savory broth, it embodies the era's fusion cuisine. Claiborne's culinary legacy, marked by his insatiable curiosity, resonates in this inspired recipe, inviting us to savor the flavors that captivated the 1960s culinary scene and forever changed how Americans approached food and dining.

Ingredients

- 2 cans (10 oz each) chopped clams, drained (reserve juice)
- 8 oz linguine or chow mein noodles, cooked
- 2 tablespoons vegetable oil
- 1 onion, thinly sliced
- 2 celery stalks, julienned
- 1 red bell pepper, thinly sliced
- 2 cloves garlic, minced
- 1 cup clam juice (reserved from canned clams)
- 1/4 cup soy sauce
- 2 tablespoons oyster sauce
- 1 tablespoon cornstarch, dissolved in - 2 tablespoons water
- Green onions and sesame seeds for garnish

Instructions

1. Sauté onions, celery, and red bell pepper in oil.

2. Add garlic and drained clams.

3. In a bowl, mix clam juice, soy sauce, and oyster sauce.

4. Pour the sauce mixture into the pan, stir in cornstarch mixture, and cook until thickened.

5. Add cooked noodles and toss.

6. Garnish with green onions and sesame seeds.

The Gourmet Revolution (1960s)

Craig Claiborne Inspired:
Harlem Renaissance Spiced Sweet Potato Casserole

Our "Craig Claiborne Inspired Harlem Renaissance Spiced Sweet Potato Casserole" pays homage to the rich culinary heritage of the Harlem Renaissance, a cultural and artistic movement in the 1920s. Claiborne, with his passion for diverse flavors, embodies the spirit of this earlier era. This spiced sweet potato casserole is a symphony of aromatic spices, marrying cinnamon, nutmeg, and allspice with creamy sweet potatoes. Layered with a brown sugar and pecan streusel, it captures the warmth and soul of Harlem's vibrant food scene during the Renaissance. Claiborne's influence in celebrating cultural diversity and distinctive flavors resonates in this inspired dish, inviting you to experience the essence of Harlem's culinary renaissance with every delicious bite.

Ingredients

- 4 large sweet potatoes, peeled and mashed
- 1/2 cup unsalted butter, melted
- 1/2 cup brown sugar
- 2 large eggs, beaten
- 1/2 cup milk
- 1 teaspoon vanilla extract

Spice Blend:
- 1 teaspoon ground cinnamon
- 1/2 teaspoon ground nutmeg
- 1/2 teaspoon ground allspice
- 1/4 teaspoon salt

Streusel Topping:
- 1/2 cup chopped pecans
- 1/4 cup all-purpose flour
- 1/4 cup brown sugar
- 2 tablespoons unsalted butter, melted

Instructions

1. Mix mashed sweet potatoes, melted butter, brown sugar, beaten eggs, milk, and vanilla.

2. Add spice blend: cinnamon, nutmeg, allspice, and salt.

3. Transfer the mixture to a baking dish.

4. Combine pecans, flour, brown sugar, and melted butter for streusel; sprinkle on top.

5. Bake at 350°F for 30-35 minutes until golden.

The Gourmet Revolution (1960s)

Paul Bocuse Inspired:
Bouillabaisse-Inspired Seafood Stew

In the dynamic culinary landscape of the 1960s, Paul Bocuse, a luminary of French gastronomy, played an important role. Renowned for his innovation and dedication to preserving traditional French cuisine, Bocuse's influence extended globally. Our "Paul Bocuse Inspired Bouillabaisse-Inspired Seafood Stew" pays homage to his legacy. Bocuse's commitment to highlighting regional ingredients is evident in this dish, a symphony of flavors reminiscent of the Mediterranean. Brimming with an array of fresh seafood, aromatic herbs, and saffron-infused broth, it captures the essence of Bocuse's culinary mastery. The stew's rich, savory profile reflects Bocuse's timeless approach, melding innovation with respect for culinary heritage. Through this inspired recipe, we invite you to savor the culinary brilliance of Paul Bocuse and immerse yourself in the sophistication and depth that defined the 1960s culinary scene.

Ingredients

- 1 lb mixed seafood (shrimp, mussels, fish fillets)
- 1 onion, finely chopped
- 2 tomatoes, diced
- 3 cloves garlic, minced
- 1 fennel bulb, sliced
- 1 leek, sliced
- 1 cup fish stock
- 1 cup white wine
- 1/4 teaspoon saffron threads
- 1 bay leaf
- 2 tablespoons olive oil
- Salt and pepper to taste
- Fresh parsley for garnish

Instructions

1. Sauté onions, garlic, fennel, and leek.

2. Add tomatoes, saffron, and bay leaf.

3. Pour in fish stock and white wine; bring to a simmer.

4. Add mixed seafood; simmer until cooked.

5. Season with salt and pepper.

6. Garnish with fresh parsley.

7. Ladle into bowls.

The Gourmet Revolution (1960s)

Paul Bocuse Inspired:
Salade Lyonnaise

Our Paul Bocuse-inspired Salade Lyonnaise transports you to the heart of the 1960s culinary renaissance. A culinary icon of the era, Bocuse's dedication to traditional French fare shines in this dish, symbolizing the revival of classic bistro culture. Crispy frisée lettuce, lardons, and a perfectly poached egg elegantly come together, showcasing the simplicity and sophistication that defined 1960s French cuisine. The interplay of textures and flavors mirrors the era's emphasis on quality ingredients and expert craftsmanship. As you savor this culinary masterpiece, you're not just indulging in a salad; you're experiencing a slice of the 1960s, where Bocuse's influence on French gastronomy resonated, paving the way for a renaissance that celebrated the timeless elegance of French culinary traditions.

Ingredients

- 1 head frisée lettuce, torn into bite-sized pieces
- 150g lardons (thick-cut bacon strips)
- 4 large eggs
- 1 tablespoon Dijon mustard
- 2 tablespoons red wine vinegar
- 1/4 cup extra-virgin olive oil
- Salt and pepper to taste
- Croutons (optional, for added crunch)

Instructions

1. Tear frisée and dress with Dijon-red wine vinaigrette.

2. Create lardons by cooking thick-cut bacon strips until crisp; drain excess fat. Break or cut to preferred size.

3. Poach eggs until yolks are runny.

4. Toss frisée with lardons.

5. Top with poached eggs.

6. Optionally, add croutons for extra crunch.

The Gourmet Revolution (1960s)

Madhur Jaffrey Inspired:
Chana Masala Stuffed Bell Peppers

Madhur Jaffrey, a trailblazing figure in the culinary world, emerged as a beacon of Indian cuisine in the 1960s U.S. culinary milieu. Her groundbreaking cookbook, "An Invitation to Indian Cooking" (1973), introduced Americans to the rich tapestry of Indian flavors and techniques. Jaffrey's approachable style and genuine passion for the cuisine made her a culinary icon, contributing significantly to the popularization of Indian food in the West.

In homage to Jaffrey's impactful legacy, our Chana Masala Stuffed Bell Peppers recipe combines the vibrancy of her flavors with a contemporary twist. Infused with aromatic spices, hearty chickpeas, and a medley of vegetables, the dish pays homage to Jaffrey's commitment to making Indian cooking accessible. These stuffed bell peppers encapsulate the essence of her culinary influence, inviting a taste of authentic Indian flavors into modern kitchens, further extending the reach of Jaffrey's culinary legacy.

Ingredients

- 4 large bell peppers, halved and seeds removed
- 1 cup dry chickpeas (soaked overnight) or canned chickpeas, drained
- 1 large onion, finely chopped
- 2 tomatoes, chopped
- 3 cloves garlic, minced
- 1-inch ginger, grated
- 1 teaspoon cumin seeds
- 1 teaspoon ground coriander
- 1 teaspoon ground cumin
- 1 teaspoon garam masala
- 1/2 teaspoon turmeric powder
- 1/2 teaspoon red chili powder (adjust to taste)
- Salt to taste
- Fresh cilantro for garnish
- Cooking oil

Instructions

1. Sauté onions, garlic, and ginger in oil.

2. Add cumin seeds, ground coriander, cumin, garam masala, turmeric, red chili, and salt.

3. Stir in chopped tomatoes, cook into a thick masala.

4. Combine with cooked chickpeas.

5. Stuff bell peppers.

6. Bake at 375°F for 25-30 mins.

7. Garnish with cilantro.

Optionally, for a traditional touch, consider using mustard oil in the initial sauté for an authentic Indian flavor.

The Gourmet Revolution (1960s)

Madhur Jaffrey Inspired:
Tandoori Chicken Skewers

Elevate your culinary experience with Madhur Jaffrey-inspired Tandoori Chicken Skewers, a testament to her mastery in Indian cuisine. Succulent chicken pieces marinated in a blend of aromatic spices, including cumin, coriander, and garam masala, evoke the essence of traditional tandoori flavors. Threaded onto skewers and grilled to perfection, the smoky char complements the vibrant spices. Accompanying this culinary delight is a refreshing Mint Yogurt Sauce, a signature touch from Jaffrey's repertoire, adding a cooling contrast to the bold spices. Immerse yourself in the rich tapestry of Indian flavors as you savor these skewers, celebrating the culinary finesse inspired by Madhur Jaffrey's dedication to authentic and delightful Indian cuisine.

Ingredients

- 1.5 lbs chicken thighs, cut into bite-sized pieces
- 1 cup plain yogurt
- 2 tablespoons Tandoori *masala*
- 1 tablespoon ground cumin
- 1 tablespoon ground coriander
- 1 teaspoon *garam masala*
- 1 teaspoon turmeric powder
- 1 tablespoon ginger-garlic paste
- Salt to taste
- Skewers, soaked in water

Mint Yogurt Sauce:
- 1 cup plain yogurt
- 1/4 cup fresh mint leaves, finely chopped
- 1 tablespoon fresh cilantro, finely chopped
- 1 teaspoon cumin powder
- Salt to taste

Instructions

1. Marinate 1.5 lbs chicken overnight: Mix 1 cup yogurt, 2 tbsp Tandoori masala, 1 tbsp cumin, 1 tbsp coriander, 1 tsp garam masala, 1 tsp turmeric, 1 tbsp ginger-garlic paste, and salt.

2. Thread marinated chicken onto soaked skewers.

3. Grill until charred and fully cooked.

The Gourmet Revolution (1960s)

Salt, Pepper & *Pasilla* Buffalo Wings

Buffalo wings, an iconic American dish, boast roots dating back to the Anchor Bar in Buffalo, New York, during the 1960s. According to legend, Teressa Bellissimo, the bar's co-owner, crafted this now-famous snack by deep-frying chicken wings and tossing them in a concoction of homemade hot sauce, butter, and vinegar. The dish swiftly gained popularity, transitioning from a late-night treat at the Anchor Bar to a culinary phenomenon throughout Buffalo and beyond. Originally introduced as a late-night indulgence, buffalo wings rapidly earned a place on restaurant menus, sports bars, and kitchen tables across the nation.

Buffalo wings, an iconic American dish, have evolved with various sauce variations, solidifying their status in American culinary culture. Often enjoyed during sporting events and social gatherings, they embody the spirit of flavorful innovation and communal enjoyment.

Ingredients

For Baking:
- Chicken wings
- Salt
- Ground black pepper
- Ground *pasilla* pepper

For Frying:
- Peanut oil

For Hot Sauce and Butter:
- Frank's RedHot Sauce
- Unsalted butter

For Serving:
- Blue cheese Dressing or, Ranch Dressing

Instructions

1. Bake wings for approx one hour at 300°F with salt, black pepper, and *pasilla*.

2. Cool thoroughly but do not freeze.

3. Fry wings to crispiness.

4. Mix Frank's RedHot with melted butter.

5. Toss wings in the sauce.

6. Serve with blue cheese or ranch dressing.

The Me Generation (1970s)

Tassajara Inspired:
Zen Macrobiotic Bowl

Tassajara, a Zen Buddhist monastery in California, profoundly influenced the culinary landscape of the 1970s. Rooted in Japanese Zen practices, Tassajara embraced a mindful and natural approach to food. With influences from macrobiotic principles, emphasizing balance and whole foods, Tassajara became a haven for vegetarian and health-conscious eating. The monastery's emphasis on simplicity, locally sourced ingredients, and self-sufficiency in the kitchen resonated with the counterculture of the era. Presenting a Tassajara Inspired Zen Macrobiotic Bowl pays homage to this influential culinary philosophy. This nourishing bowl reflects Tassajara's commitment to harmonizing flavors, fostering well-being, and epitomizing the mindful and holistic spirit that captivated the 1970s food scene. It serves as a delicious reminder of the era's exploration of diverse, health-focused, and spiritually rooted culinary practices.

Ingredients

- 1 cup short-grain brown rice
- 1 cup steamed cauliflower florets
- 1/2 cup shredded carrots
- 1/2 cup sautéed mustard greens
- 1/4 cup sliced radishes
- 1/4 cup chopped green onions
- 1/4 cup tamari-roasted sunflower seeds
- 1 tablespoon sesame oil
- 2 tablespoons brown rice vinegar
Salt and pepper to taste

Instructions

1. Cook brown rice and place rice in bowls.

3. Add steamed cauliflower.

4. Top with shredded carrots.

5. Sauté mustard greens and add to bowls.

6. Garnish with radishes and green onions.

7. Drizzle with sesame oil and vinegar.

8. Sprinkle tamari-roasted sunflower seeds.

9. Season with salt and pepper.

10. Gently toss.

11. Serve!

The Me Generation (1970s)

Moosewood inspired:
Chocolate Zucchini Power Clusters

In the 1970s, Moosewood, epitomized by the iconic Moosewood Cookbook, emerged as a pioneering force in the culinary landscape. Authored by Mollie Katzen, the cookbook reflected the era's growing interest in vegetarianism and whole foods. Moosewood's recipes celebrated simplicity, emphasizing fresh, local ingredients and innovative vegetarian dishes. In this spirit, our Moosewood-inspired power cluster recipe pays homage to that era's ethos. Combining grated zucchini, rolled oats, almond butter, honey, and cocoa powder, these clusters offer a nutrient-packed, energy-boosting treat. Just as Moosewood championed accessible, plant-based cuisine, these power clusters seamlessly blend wholesome ingredients, nodding to the bygone era's culinary trends while providing a delicious and health-conscious snack for today's palate.

Ingredients

- 1 cup grated zucchini (excess moisture squeezed out)
- 1 cup rolled oats
- 1/2 cup almond butter or peanut butter
- 1/4 cup honey or maple syrup
- 1/4 cup unsweetened cocoa powder
- 1/2 teaspoon vanilla extract
- A pinch of salt
- Optional add-ins: chopped nuts, seeds, dried fruits, or chocolate chips

Instructions

1. Grate and squeeze moisture from 1 cup zucchini.

2. Mix zucchini with 1 cup oats, 1/2 cup almond butter, 1/4 cup honey, 1/4 cup cocoa powder, 1/2 tsp vanilla, and a pinch of salt.

3. Optionally, add nuts, seeds, or chocolate chips.

4. Shape the mixture into clusters.

5. Chill for 30 mins.

6. Enjoy these Moosewood-inspired power-packed treats!

The Me Generation (1970s)

Alice Waters Inspired:
Seasonal Stonefruit Galette

Alice Waters, a culinary luminary in the 1970s, revolutionized American cuisine through her farm-to-table philosophy, advocating for fresh, local ingredients. As the founder of Chez Panisse in 1971, Waters championed seasonal cooking, inspiring a generation to appreciate the purity of flavors. In homage to her influence, our Alice Waters-inspired recipe, the Seasonal Stonefruit Galette, captures the essence of Chez Panisse. Using locally-sourced, ripe stonefruits like peaches or plums, the galette embodies Waters' dedication to simplicity and quality. The flaky, homemade crust highlights the natural sweetness of the fruits, celebrating the harmony of seasonal ingredients. This galette not only pays homage to Waters' culture-changing culinary contributions but also brings the farm-fresh ethos of the 1970s into contemporary kitchens.

Ingredients

- 1 1/2 cups all-purpose flour
- 1/2 cup unsalted butter, cold and cubed
- 2 tablespoons granulated sugar
- 1/4 teaspoon salt
- 3-4 tablespoons ice water

Filling:
- 4-5 cups seasonal stonefruits (peaches, plums, etc.), sliced
- 1/4 cup granulated sugar (adjust based on fruit sweetness)
- 1 tablespoon lemon juice
- Zest of one lemon
- 2 tablespoons apricot jam (for glaze)

Instructions

1. Pulse crust ingredients in a food processor.

2. Toss stone fruits with sugar and lemon.

3. Roll out the crust.

4. Fill the crust with the fruit mixture.

5. Fold the crust over the top of the filling.

6. Bake at 375°F.

7. Glaze with warmed apricot jam.

The Me Generation (1970s)

Alice Waters Inspired:
Herb-Infused Quiche

In homage to Alice Waters' culinary philosophy, our "Alice Waters Inspired: Herb-Infused Quiche" pays tribute to her dedication to fresh, locally sourced ingredients. This original recipe combines a flaky homemade crust with a luscious filling of locally procured eggs, cream, and an array of fresh herbs like thyme, rosemary, and chives. Inspired by Waters' farm-to-table ethos, the quiche becomes a canvas for showcasing the purity of each ingredient. Baked to golden perfection, the Herb-Infused Quiche captures the essence of simplicity and sophistication championed by Waters. With each bite, savor the harmonious blend of herbs, creating a culinary masterpiece that mirrors the spirit of Chez Panisse in the comfort of your home. This quiche not only honors Waters' timeless influence but also invites you to partake in a delicious journey through the flavors of locally inspired, herb-infused goodness.

Ingredients

For the Crust:
- 1 1/4 cups all-purpose flour
- 1/2 cup unsalted butter, chilled and cubed
- 1/4 teaspoon salt
- 3-4 tablespoons ice water

For the Filling:
- 4 large eggs
- 1 cup heavy cream
- Salt and black pepper, to taste
- 1 tablespoon fresh thyme, chopped
- 1 tablespoon fresh rosemary, chopped
- 2 tablespoons fresh chives, finely chopped
- 1 cup gruyere or your preferred cheese, shredded

Instructions

For Crust:
1. Preheat the oven to 375°F (190°C).
2. Pulse 1 1/4 cups flour, 1/2 cup butter, pinch of salt.
3. Add 3-4 tbsp ice water.
4. Shape the dough, chill, and roll it to line the pie dish.
5. Blind bake the crust for 15 minutes.

For Quiche:
6. Whisk 4 eggs, 1 cup cream, salt, and pepper.
7. Stir in 1 tbsp thyme, 1 tbsp rosemary, 2 tbsp chives, and 1 cup shredded Gruyere.
8. Pour the mixture into the pre-baked crust.
9. Bake at 375°F for 30-35 mins.

The Me Generation (1970s)

Marcella Hazan Inspired:
Almond Tiramisu

In the 1970s, Marcella Hazan, an influential Italian culinary authority, reshaped American perceptions of Italian cuisine. Her emphasis on simplicity and quality ingredients revolutionized home cooking, making authentic Italian flavors accessible. In homage to Hazan's legacy, our MH-Inspired: Original Almond Tiramisu celebrates the essence of her teachings. This exquisite dessert combines layers of delicate almond-flavored sponge cake, rich mascarpone, and a hint of espresso. The recipe pays homage to Hazan's commitment to preserving the integrity of traditional Italian dishes while incorporating a unique twist. As you savor each bite of this Almond Tiramisu, you embark on a culinary journey that encapsulates Hazan's timeless influence, bringing the warmth and authenticity of Italian kitchens to your home. It's a delightful tribute to a culinary pioneer whose impact endures through the flavors she introduced to the American table.

Ingredients

For the Almond Sponge:
- 3/4 cup almond flour
- 1/2 cup all-purpose flour
- 1 teaspoon baking powder
- Pinch of salt
- 3 large eggs
- 1/2 cup granulated sugar
- 1 teaspoon almond extract

For the Tiramisu:
- 1 cup strong espresso, cooled
- 1/4 cup amaretto liqueur
- 1 cup mascarpone cheese
- 1/2 cup heavy cream
- 1/4 cup powdered sugar
- Cocoa powder for dusting

Instructions

1. Blend almond flour, all-purpose flour, baking powder, and salt for the almond sponge.
2. Beat eggs and sugar, add almond extract, and fold in dry ingredients.
3. Bake until golden, then cut into squares.
4. In a dish, blend espresso with amaretto.
5. Dip almond squares in the espresso-amaretto mixture and layer them.
6. Whisk mascarpone until smooth.
7. Whip heavy cream with powdered sugar until stiff peaks form.
8. Fold whipped cream into mascarpone.
9. Spread half of the mixture over the sponge layer.
10. Repeat with another layer of dipped sponge.
11. Top with the remaining mascarpone cream.
12. Refrigerate for at least 4 hours or overnight.
13. Dust the top with cocoa powder before serving.

Marcella Hazan Inspired:
Slow-Cooked Tomato Sauce with Onion and Butter

Embrace the convenience of modern cooking with a slow cooker twist on the classic Marcella Hazan-inspired Slow Cooked Tomato Sauce with Onion and Butter. In this original approach, the slow cooker becomes the culinary maestro, melding the flavors to perfection over an extended simmer. Begin by layering the slow cooker with ripe tomatoes, aromatic onions, and a generous dollop of butter. Allow the ingredients to harmonize over hours, releasing rich, velvety notes that pay homage to Hazan's traditional recipe. The slow cooker method intensifies the sauce's depth, creating a luscious, melt-in-your-mouth experience. As the fragrance permeates your kitchen, you'll appreciate the fusion of timeless Italian flavors with the contemporary ease of slow cooking. This original adaptation invites you to savor the essence of Hazan's culinary legacy in a convenient, flavorful, and time-honored Tomato Sauce with Onion and Butter.

Ingredients

- 8-10 ripe tomatoes, peeled and chopped
- 1 large onion, peeled and halved
- 1/2 cup unsalted butter
- Salt, to taste

Instructions

1. Place 8-10 ripe, peeled, chopped tomatoes in a slow cooker.

2. Add 1 halved onion and 1/2 cup butter.

3. Cook on low for 6-8 hours, stirring occasionally.

4. Season with salt halfway through.

5. Discard onion before serving.

6. Use the rich, slow-cooked sauce on pasta or pizza, capturing the essence of Marcella Hazan's classic recipe with a modern twist.

The Me Generation (1970s)

Jacques Pépin Inspired:
Chicken Liver Pâté

In the culinary landscape of the 1970s, the influential Jacques Pépin emerged as a maestro of French cuisine, reshaping American kitchens with his innovative and accessible approach. Our Chicken Liver Pâté, inspired by Pépin's culinary finesse during this era, reflects his commitment to elevating flavors with simplicity. Combining chicken livers, butter, and aromatic herbs, this recipe captures the essence of Pépin's artistry, echoing the gastronomic sophistication he brought to American audiences. As Pépin left an indelible mark on 1970s culinary culture, our homage invites you to savor the timeless flavors that defined this era, celebrating a culinary pioneer whose influence transcends decades and continues to inspire a love for French gastronomy.

Ingredients

- 1 pound chicken livers, trimmed
- 1 cup unsalted butter
- 1 large Spanish or Vidalia onion, or two medium shallots, finely chopped
- 2 cloves garlic, minced
- 1/4 cup brandy or cognac
- Salt and black pepper, to taste
- 1/2 teaspoon dried thyme
- 1 bay leaf
- Fresh parsley, for garnish

Instructions

1. Sauté livers until pink inside.
2. Sauté onions or shallots, garlic in butter.
3. Deglaze with brandy.
4. Add livers, salt, pepper, thyme.
5. Blend until smooth.
6. Chill.
7. Garnish with parsley.
8. Serve with bread.

The Me Generation (1970s)

Vincent Price Inspired:
Chocolate Orange Mousse

Vincent Price, celebrated for his illustrious acting career, also left an indelible mark as a culinary connoisseur and author. In the 1960s and 1970s, Price, along with his wife Mary, penned the influential cookbook "A Treasury of Great Recipes." A culinary enthusiast and advocate for gourmet dining, Price's passion extended beyond the silver screen into the kitchen.

Our original Chocolate Orange Mousse pays homage to Vincent Price's refined taste and love for the extraordinary. This luscious dessert blends the richness of dark chocolate with the vibrant zest of orange, echoing the sophistication Price often celebrated in his culinary endeavors. By crafting a dessert that combines elegance and indulgence, we tip our hat to the man whose culinary legacy transcends acting, inviting you to savor a taste inspired by the gourmet world Price so ardently explored in his books and beyond.

Ingredients

- 6 ounces dark chocolate, chopped
- 1/2 cup unsalted butter
- 3 large eggs, separated
- 1/4 cup granulated sugar
- Zest of one orange
- 1 teaspoon vanilla extract
- Pinch of salt
- Whipped cream and orange segments for garnish

Instructions

1. Melt 6 oz dark chocolate with 1/2 cup butter.

2. Beat 3 egg yolks with 1/4 cup sugar.

3. Add melted chocolate, orange zest, and vanilla.

4. Whip egg whites until stiff.

5. Gently fold into chocolate mixture.

6. Pour into glasses, chill.

7. Garnish with whipped cream and orange segments.

The Me Generation (1970s)

Shrimp Scampi

Shrimp Scampi, a dish that originated in Italy, gained popularity in the United States during the 1970s. The term "scampi" traditionally referred to a type of small lobster found in the Adriatic Sea. However, in the U.S., the dish evolved to feature large shrimp cooked in a garlic-infused butter and white wine sauce.

During the 1970s, there was a growing interest in international cuisines in the United States. Italian dishes, including Shrimp Scampi, became trendy and were embraced by home cooks and restaurants alike. The simplicity of the recipe, featuring succulent shrimp combined with garlic, butter, and wine, appealed to a wide audience. Shrimp Scampi soon became a classic and continues to be a popular seafood dish today.

The dish's rise in popularity during the 1970s reflects a broader cultural shift toward exploring and incorporating diverse culinary influences, marking an era where international flavors began to play a more prominent role in American kitchens.

Ingredients

- 1 pound large shrimp, peeled and de-veined
- 4 tablespoons unsalted butter
- 3 tablespoons olive oil
- 4 cloves garlic, minced
- 1/4 teaspoon red pepper flakes (optional)
- 1/2 cup dry white wine
- Juice of 1 lemon
- Salt and black pepper, to taste
- 2 tablespoons fresh parsley, chopped
- Cooked linguine or pasta of choice

Instructions

1. Season 1 lb peeled shrimp with salt and pepper.

2. Sauté shrimp in 2 tbsp butter and 2 tbsp olive oil until pink. Set aside.

3. In the same pan, add 2 tbsp butter and 1 tbsp olive oil.

4. Sauté 4 minced garlic cloves and optional red pepper flakes.

5. Deglaze with 1/2 cup white wine.

6. Return shrimp, add lemon juice, and toss with 2 tbsp chopped parsley.

7. Serve over cooked linguine..

The Me Generation (1970s)

Chili Con Queso

The 1970s marked a vibrant era for Tex-Mex cuisine, and one iconic dish that emerged during this time is "Chili Con Queso." This classic Tex-Mex recipe combines the bold flavors of melted cheese, spicy chilies, and savory seasonings. Originating from the fusion of Texan and Mexican culinary traditions, Chili Con Queso became a popular party and snack dish. Typically made with a blend of cheeses, diced tomatoes with green chilies, and various spices, this dip embodies the spirit of communal dining and shared flavors that defined Tex-Mex cuisine in the '70s. Serve it with tortilla chips for an authentic taste of this flavorful era, celebrating the fusion and fun that characterize Tex-Mex culinary heritage. We are going full on 70s with the addition of Velveeta Cheese in this one- store-bought & homemade options.

Ingredients

- 1 pound Velveeta cheese, cubed (a popular processed cheese in the '70s)
- 1 can (10 ounces) diced tomatoes with green chilies, undrained (e.g., Rotel)
- 1/2 cup diced onions
- 1/2 cup diced green bell peppers
- 1/2 teaspoon chili powder
- 1/4 teaspoon garlic powder
- 1/4 teaspoon ground cumin
- 1/4 teaspoon black pepper
- Tortilla chips, for serving

For Homemade 'Velveeta' Cheese:
2 cups shredded sharp cheddar cheese
1 1/2 cups whole milk
1 tablespoon unflavored gelatin
1/4 cup dry milk powder
1/2 teaspoon salt

Instructions

For Homemade 'Velveeta':
1. Combine 2 cups cheddar, 1 1/2 cups milk, 1 tbsp gelatin (bloomed in 1/4 cup milk), 1/4 cup dry milk, and 1/2 tsp salt.
2. Melt the mixture.
3. Blend until smooth.
4. Pour into a mold.
5. Refrigerate for 3-4 hours.

For Chili Con Queso
1. Dice 'Velveeta' cheese.
2. In a saucepan, melt it with diced tomatoes, onions, and green peppers.
3. Add chili powder, garlic powder, cumin, and black pepper.
4. Simmer until smooth.
5. Serve warm. with tortilla chips.

The Reagan Era (1980s)

Justin Wilson Inspired:
Cajun Cornbread Pudding

The essence of Justin Wilson, a beloved chef and TV host in the 80s, is captured in this hearty Cajun-inspired dish. Combining the rustic charm of cornbread with the bold flavors of andouille sausage, corn, and Cajun seasoning, this recipe exemplifies Wilson's passion for robust Southern cuisine. In a simple yet flavorful process, the cornbread mixture is enriched with a velvety blend of milk, beaten eggs, melted butter, and a carefully balanced Cajun seasoning. Baked to perfection, the dish emanates a golden-brown allure, promising a symphony of textures and tastes. Justin Wilson, renowned for his engaging storytelling and love for Louisiana's culinary traditions, left an indelible mark on the 80s culinary scene, inviting viewers to savor the warmth of Southern kitchens and the heartiness of its comforting fare.

Ingredients

- 2 cups cornbread, crumbled
- 1 cup andouille sausage, diced
- 1 cup corn kernels
- 1 cup grated sharp cheddar cheese
- 1 cup milk
- 3 eggs, beaten
- 1/2 cup diced green onions
- 2 tablespoons melted butter
- 1 teaspoon Cajun seasoning
- Salt and pepper to taste

Instructions

1. Preheat the oven to 350°F.

2. Mix crumbled cornbread, andouille sausage, corn, cheese, and green onions in a bowl.

3. In a separate bowl, whisk together milk, beaten eggs, melted butter, Cajun seasoning, salt, and pepper.

4. Pour the egg mixture over the cornbread mixture and stir well.

5. Transfer the mixture to a greased baking dish.

6. Bake until set and golden brown, approximately 30-40 minutes.

The Reagan Era (1980s)

Paul Prudhomme Inspired:
Cajun Blackened Fish

This Paul Prudhomme-inspired Cajun Blackened Fish recipe encapsulates the fiery essence of the legendary chef's influence on American cuisine. Prudhomme, a pioneering figure in popularizing Cajun and Creole flavors, brought his culinary mastery to kitchens nationwide. His innovative blackening technique, featuring a potent blend of spices, imbued dishes with an unmistakable smokiness.

The recipe, renowned for its bold Cajun flavors, has earned a unique reputation— igniting more fire alarms than any other in modern kitchen history. The sizzling cast-iron skillet, essential to achieve the perfect blackening, often leaves a trail of aromatic smoke that evokes both culinary excitement and a touch of chaos. Through this dish, enthusiasts experience not only the rich tapestry of Cajun cuisine but also the adventurous spirit that defines Paul Prudhomme's important culinary legacy in American kitchens.

Ingredients

- 4 fish fillets (such as redfish or catfish)
- 1/2 cup unsalted butter, melted

Cajun Blackening Spice Mix:
- 2 tablespoons paprika
- 1 tablespoon onion powder
- 1 tablespoon garlic powder
- 1 tablespoon dried thyme
- 1 teaspoon cayenne pepper
- 1 teaspoon black pepper
- 1 teaspoon white pepper
- 1 teaspoon dried oregano
- 1 teaspoon smoked paprika
- 1 teaspoon salt

Instructions

1. Dip the fish in melted butter.

2. Coat the fish generously with Cajun Blackening Spice Mix.

3. Preheat a cast-iron skillet.

4. Cook the fish for 2-3 minutes per side until blackened and cooked through.

5. Serve with lemon wedges.

The Reagan Era (1980s)

Martin Yan-Inspired:
Savory Chicken Lettuce Cups

In the vibrant culinary milieu of the 1980s, Martin Yan emerged as a dynamic force, captivating audiences with his infectious energy and expertise in Chinese cuisine. As the host of "Yan Can Cook," his television presence became iconic, introducing viewers to the artistry of wok cooking and the intricacies of Chinese culinary traditions.

This Martin Yan-inspired recipe pays homage to his legacy. The Savory Chicken Lettuce Cups embody the essence of Yan's approachable yet masterful cooking style. Ground chicken wok-cooked to perfection blends seamlessly with the crunch of water chestnuts and the earthiness of shiitake mushrooms. The soy-infused sauce, with hints of hoisin and sesame, weaves together a symphony of flavors. Served in crisp iceberg lettuce cups, this dish is a nod to Yan's dedication to making Chinese cuisine accessible and delightful to home cooks, echoing the spirit of his influential contributions to the culinary landscape of the 1980s.

Ingredients

- 1 lb ground chicken
- 1 cup water chestnuts, finely chopped
- 1/2 cup shiitake mushrooms, diced
- 1/4 cup soy sauce
- 2 tablespoons *hoisin* sauce
- 1 tablespoon sesame oil
- 1 tablespoon fresh ginger, minced
- 2 cloves garlic, minced
- 1 teaspoon sugar
- Iceberg lettuce leaves for cups
- Green onions, chopped, for garnish
- Crushed peanuts for topping

Instructions

1. Brown 1 lb ground chicken.

2. Add chopped water chestnuts, shiitake mushrooms, ginger, and garlic.

3. Stir-fry the mixture.

4. In a bowl, mix 1/4 cup soy sauce, 2 tbsp hoisin sauce, 1 tbsp sesame oil, 1 tsp sugar.

5. Pour the sauce over the chicken and stir.

6. Spoon the mixture into lettuce leaves.

7. Garnish with green onions and crushed peanuts.

The Reagan Era (1980s)

Benihana Inspired:
Japanese Clear Onion Soup

As you plan your visit to a favorite sushi or Japanese restaurant, considering teppanyaki, sashimi, or teriyaki, let's explore a dish inspired by the iconic Benihana of the 1980s. Founded by Hiroaki "Rocky" Aoki, Benihana was renowned for its theatrical hibachi grilling performances and exquisite Japanese cuisine. The Benihana-style Japanese Clear Onion Soup from that era epitomized simplicity and depth of flavor. A delicate broth, enriched with sautéed onions, carrots, and celery, served as a soothing prelude to the teppanyaki feast. Infused with garlic, ginger, soy sauce, and a touch of mirin, the soup exuded warmth and authenticity, complementing the immersive dining experience that defined Benihana in the 1980s.

Ingredients

- 1 large onion, thinly sliced
- 2 carrots, julienned
- 2 celery stalks, sliced
- 8 cups clear chicken or vegetable broth
- 1 tablespoon vegetable oil
- 2 cloves garlic, minced
- 1 teaspoon ginger, grated
- 2 tablespoons soy sauce
- 1 teaspoon mirin (optional)
- Salt and pepper to taste
- Green onions, thinly sliced, for garnish

Instructions

1. Sauté garlic, ginger, onions, carrots, and celery.

2. Add clear broth, soy sauce, mirin.

3. Simmer for 15-20 mins.

4. Season with salt and pepper.

5. Optional: strain for clarity.

6. Garnish with green onions.

The Reagan Era (1980s)

Wolfgang Puck Inspired:
Grilled Eggplant Lasagna Rolls

In the vibrant culinary landscape of the 1980s, Wolfgang Puck emerged as a trailblazing chef, reshaping American gastronomy with his innovative approach. Inspired by Puck's commitment to fresh, seasonal ingredients and bold flavor combinations at Spago, the Grilled Eggplant Lasagna Rolls pay homage to this era of culinary experimentation.

The dish encapsulates Puck's Californian influence, using grilled eggplant in lieu of traditional pasta for a lighter twist on classic lasagna. The marriage of creamy ricotta, savory mozzarella, and Parmesan, combined with the smoky essence of grilled eggplant, creates a flavor symphony that mirrors Puck's dedication to culinary artistry. These rolls, bathed in marinara sauce and garnished with basil, represent a culinary nod to the 1980s, a time when Wolfgang Puck's culinary innovations left an indelible mark on American cuisine.

Ingredients

- 2 large eggplants, sliced lengthwise
- Olive oil for brushing
- Salt and black pepper to taste

For the Filling:
- 1 cup ricotta cheese
- 1 cup shredded mozzarella cheese
- 1/2 cup grated Parmesan cheese
- 1 cup fresh spinach, chopped
- 2 cloves garlic, minced
- Salt and black pepper to taste

For Assembly:
- 2 cups marinara sauce
- Fresh basil leaves for garnish
- Additional Parmesan for sprinkling

Instructions

1. Brush eggplant with olive oil, grill until tender.

2. Mix ricotta, mozzarella, Parmesan, spinach, garlic, salt, and pepper.

3. Spread filling on eggplant slices, roll.

4. Place rolls seam-side down in a baking dish.

5. Top with marinara and Parmesan.

6. Bake at 375°F for 20-25 mins.

The Reagan Era (1980s)

Nick Malgieri Inspired:
Pistachio-Raspberry Linzer Torte

Nick Malgieri, a prominent pastry chef in the 1980s, influenced the culinary world with his emphasis on classic baking techniques and high-quality ingredients. While specific recipes from that era might not be available, the Walnut-Raspberry or Pistachio-Raspberry Linzer Torte presented here draws inspiration from Malgieri's principles. The simplicity of the recipe mirrors the elegant and timeless approach often favored by chefs in the 1980s. The choice of walnuts or pistachios in the crust aligns with the era's trend of incorporating different nuts into desserts. Raspberry jam preserves the traditional essence of a Linzer Torte, resulting in a harmonious blend of flavors and textures. Although not directly from Malgieri, this recipe pays homage to his culinary philosophy and captures the spirit of classic 1980s desserts with a modern twist.

Ingredients

For the crust:
- 1 cup all-purpose flour
- 1 cup chopped walnuts or shelled pistachios (finely ground)
- 1/2 cup unsalted butter, softened
- 1/2 cup granulated sugar
- 1 teaspoon vanilla extract
- 1/2 teaspoon almond extract (optional, or you can use vanilla extract)
- 1/4 teaspoon salt

For the filling:
- 1/2 cup raspberry jam or preserves

For topping:
- Powdered sugar for dusting

Instructions

1. Combine 1 cup flour, 1 cup finely ground walnuts or pistachios, 1/2 cup softened butter, 1/2 cup sugar, 1 tsp vanilla, 1/2 tsp almond extract (optional), and 1/4 tsp salt for the crust.

2. Press 2/3 of the dough into a greased tart pan.

3. Spread 1/2 cup raspberry jam.

4. Roll remaining dough into strips for lattice top.

5. Bake at 350°F for 25-30 mins.

6. Cool before removing from the pan.

7. Dust with powdered sugar.

8. Slice and enjoy!

The Reagan Era (1980s)

Baked Brie

In the culinary landscape of the 1980s, the popularity of baked brie soared to new heights, marking an era where sophisticated appetizers gained widespread appreciation. Brie, alongside its cousin Camembert, stood out as the epitome of European elegance in American households. Remarkably, the supermarket shelves primarily showcased domestic cheeses, making the discovery of imported brie and Camembert in metal cans a memorable experience!

These soft and creamy French cheeses, encased in a convenient tin, became a symbol of gourmet indulgence. Baked brie emerged as a star hors d'oeuvre, wrapped in flaky puff pastry and adorned with fruit preserves or nuts. As the 1980s embraced culinary experimentation, the ritual of unveiling a warm, gooey wheel of brie marked a cultural shift towards embracing international flavors, forever shaping the appetizer landscape.

Ingredients

- 1 wheel of Brie cheese (about 8-12 ounces)
- 1 sheet of puff pastry (thawed if using frozen)
- 1/4 cup fruit preserves (apricot, raspberry, or fig work well)
- 1/4 cup chopped nuts (walnuts, almonds, or pecans)
- 1 egg (beaten, for egg wash)
- Crackers or baguette slices (for serving)

Instructions

1. Heat your oven to 375°F (190°C).
2. Roll out puff pastry on a floured surface. Put Brie in the center.
3. Spread fruit preserves and sprinkle nuts on the Brie.
4. Fold pastry edges over, seal, and flip with seam down.
5. Put on parchment paper-lined sheet.
6. Brush the pastry with beaten egg for a golden finish.
7. Bake for 20-25 mins until golden.
8. Let it cool a bit after removing from the oven.
9. Serve with crackers or baguette slices.

The Reagan Era (1980s)

Turkey Enchilada with Mole Sauce

In the 1980s Mexican restaurant scene, the Turkey Enchilada with Mole Sauce emerged as a groundbreaking dish, epitomizing the era's fusion of traditional Mexican flavors with innovative culinary twists. This enchilada, filled with succulent turkey and bathed in rich, complex mole sauce, marked a departure from more familiar protein options.

Mole sauce, with its intricate blend of chili peppers, spices, and surprising touch of chocolate, challenged and ultimately expanded the American palate. This shockingly new approach to chocolate showcased its versatility beyond desserts, introducing diners to a savory, nuanced experience. The Turkey Enchilada with Mole Sauce became a symbol of the evolving Mexican culinary landscape, where chefs embraced bold experimentation, blending authenticity with contemporary creativity. The dish, reflective of the 1980s dining ethos, not only delighted taste buds but also played a pivotal role in broadening the cultural appreciation of Mexican cuisine in the United States.

Ingredients

Oaxaca cheese or sharp Cheddar

For the Turkey:
- 3 cups shredded cooked turkey
- 1 onion, finely diced
- 2 cloves garlic, minced
- 1 teaspoon ground cumin
- 1 teaspoon chili powder
- Salt and pepper to taste
- 1 tablespoon vegetable oil

For the Mole Sauce:
- 3 tablespoons vegetable oil
- 1/3 cup chili powder
- 1/4 cup all-purpose flour
- 1/4 cup cocoa powder
- 1 teaspoon ground cinnamon
- 1 teaspoon ground coriander
- 1/2 teaspoon smoked paprika
- 3 cups chicken broth
- 1/4 cup tomato paste
- 2 tablespoons almond butter
- 2 ounces dark chocolate, chopped

Instructions

Make mole sauce:
1. In a saucepan, heat vegetable oil over medium heat. Add chili powder, flour, cocoa powder, cinnamon, coriander, and smoked paprika. Stir continuously for 2-3 minutes until fragrant.

2. Gradually whisk in chicken broth to create a smooth mixture.

3. Add tomato paste, almond butter, and dark chocolate. Stir until the chocolate is melted, and the sauce is well combined, and simmer the sauce over low heat for 10-15 minutes, allowing it to thicken.

For the Enchilada
Sauté turkey and turkey spices quickly in oil. Roll in tortillas with cheese. Pour mole sauce over enchiladas. Bake at 375°F for 20-25 mins. Garnish with cilantro.

The Reagan Era (1980s)

Basil Pesto Sun-Dried Tomato Spinach Dip

In the 1980s, spinach dip rose to culinary stardom as a quintessential party appetizer, encapsulating the era's casual entertaining spirit. Typically featuring chopped spinach, mayonnaise, sour cream, and water chestnuts, it became a beloved classic at social gatherings.

Fast forward to the present, the Basil Pesto Sun-Dried Tomato Spinach Dip offers a contemporary twist on this iconic dish. By incorporating sun-dried tomatoes and basil pesto, this updated recipe elevates the dip with a vibrant fusion of flavors. The creamy texture, coupled with the sweet intensity of sun-dried tomatoes and the herbaceous kick of basil, makes it a versatile and crowd-pleasing option for today's modern palate, seamlessly blending nostalgia with contemporary culinary preferences.

Ingredients

- 1 cup frozen chopped spinach, thawed and drained
- 1/2 cup sun-dried tomatoes, finely chopped
- 1/2 cup mayonnaise
- 1/2 cup sour cream or Greek yogurt
- 1/2 cup grated Parmesan cheese
- 1/4 cup basil pesto
- 1 clove garlic, minced
- Salt and pepper to taste
- 1/4 cup pine nuts, toasted (optional, for garnish)

Instructions

1. In a bowl, combine thawed, drained spinach with finely chopped sun-dried tomatoes.

2. In another bowl, mix mayonnaise, sour cream or Greek yogurt, grated Parmesan, and basil pesto.

3. Add minced garlic, salt, and pepper to the creamy mixture.

4. Combine the creamy mixture with the spinach and tomatoes.

5. Transfer the mixture to a baking dish and bake at 375°F for 20-25 minutes until bubbly and golden.

6. Optionally, toast pine nuts and sprinkle for added crunch and flavor.

7. Allow the dip to cool slightly before serving.

The Reagan Era (1980s)

Quick Boozy Beef Stroganoff

In the 1980s, Beef Stroganoff epitomized comforting and indulgent dining, often served with tender strips of beef enveloped in a rich, creamy sauce, becoming a staple on family tables and restaurant menus alike. Fast forward to today, the Cognac or Brandy Beef Stroganoff recipe pays homage to the classic while infusing a touch of sophistication. Thin slices of beef are seared to perfection, and a velvety sauce is crafted with a delightful blend of cognac, tomato paste, and Dijon mustard. The result is a dish that offers a harmonious marriage of savory flavors with a hint of warmth from the brandy. Enhanced by earthy mushrooms and the creaminess of sour cream, this modern twist elevates Beef Stroganoff to a luxurious dining experience, perfect for relishing the timeless and comforting essence of the 1980s in a contemporary setting.

Ingredients

- 1.5 lbs (680g) beef sirloin or tenderloin, thinly sliced
- Salt and pepper to taste
- 2 tablespoons olive oil
- 1 onion, finely chopped
- 3 cloves garlic, minced
- 8 oz (225g) cremini or button mushrooms, sliced
- 2 tablespoons all-purpose flour
- 2 tablespoons tomato paste
- 1/4 cup cognac or brandy
- 1 cup beef broth
- 1 tablespoon Worcestershire sauce
- 1 teaspoon Dijon mustard
- 1/2 cup sour cream
- Fresh parsley, chopped, for garnish
- Egg noodles or rice, for serving

Instructions

1. Season and sear thinly sliced beef.
2. Sauté onions, garlic, and mushrooms.
3. Sprinkle with flour, add tomato paste.
4. Pour in cognac or brandy to deglaze.
5. Stir in broth, Worcestershire, and Dijon.
6. Simmer, return beef, cook until thickened.
7. Stir in sour cream, avoid boiling.
8. Adjust seasoning.
9. Serve over noodles or rice, garnish with parsley.

The Digital Age (1990s)

Jean-Georges Vongerichten Inspired:
Chili-Lime Shrimp Tacos and Avocado Crema

In the culinary landscape of the 1990s, Jean-Georges Vongerichten stood as a trailblazer, renowned for his innovative global cuisine. His influence is evident in the modern take on his style with the Chili-Lime Shrimp Tacos and Avocado *Crema*. Drawing inspiration from Vongerichten's bold flavor combinations, these tacos feature succulent shrimp marinated in zesty chili and lime. The dish is elevated with a cooling avocado *crema*, blending creamy avocado with tangy yogurt and aromatic cilantro. This recipe reflects Vongerichten's commitment to creating dishes that marry diverse elements, offering a harmonious balance of heat, acidity, and richness. The Chili-Lime Shrimp Tacos with Avocado *Crema* pay homage to the culinary spirit of the 1990s while embracing the contemporary preference for vibrant, globally influenced flavors.

Ingredients

For the Shrimp Marinade:
- 1 lb large shrimp, peeled and de-veined
- 2 tablespoons olive oil
- 2 tablespoons fresh lime juice
- 1 teaspoon cascabel chili powder (plus extra for sprinkling)
- 1 teaspoon ground cumin
- Salt and pepper to taste

For the Avocado Crema:
- 2 ripe avocados, peeled and pitted
- 1/2 cup Greek yogurt
- 1/4 cup fresh cilantro, chopped
- 1 tablespoon lime juice
- Salt to taste

For Assembly:
Corn tortillas
Shredded cabbage
Fresh cilantro leaves
Lime wedges

Instructions

1. Marinate shrimp in a mix of olive oil, lime juice, cascabel chili powder, cumin, salt, and pepper.

2. Blend avocados, Greek yogurt, cilantro, lime juice, and salt for the crema.

3. Cook the shrimp until opaque.

4. Warm tortillas.

5. Assemble tacos with avocado crema, shrimp, shredded cabbage, and cilantro.

6. Sprinkle extra cascabel chili powder.

7. Serve with lime wedges.

The Digital Age (1990s)

Gordan Ramsey (90s-version) Inspired:
Vegetable Wellington

In the culinary landscape of the 1990s, Gordon Ramsay emerged as a formidable force, showcasing his culinary prowess and exacting standards. This original Vegetable Wellington pays homage to Ramsay's classic techniques and bold flavors. The finely chopped medley of mushrooms, spinach, and grated vegetables, sautéed with aromatic thyme and encased in golden puff pastry, reflects Ramsay's commitment to elevated and skillfully crafted dishes.

Inspired by his precision and dedication to quality, this vegetarian masterpiece transforms humble ingredients into a show-stopping entrée. The layers of flavor and the golden, crispy exterior, brushed with Dijon mustard, embody Ramsay's timeless influence, offering a contemporary take on his 1990s culinary legacy. In every bite, the Vegetable Wellington captures the essence of Ramsay's culinary artistry and brings a touch of sophistication to the table.

Ingredients

For the Filling:
- 2 cups mixed mushrooms (button, cremini, or shiitake), finely chopped
- 1 cup spinach, chopped
- 1 large carrot, grated
- 1 small zucchini, grated
- 1 onion, finely chopped
- 3 cloves garlic, minced
- 1 tablespoon olive oil
- 1 teaspoon thyme, chopped
- Salt and pepper to taste

For Assembly:
- Puff pastry sheets
- Dijon mustard (for brushing)
- 1 egg (for egg wash)

Instructions

1. Sauté onions and garlic in olive oil.

2. Add mushrooms, carrot, zucchini, and spinach.

3. Season with thyme, salt, and pepper.

4. Roll out puff pastry, brush with Dijon.

5. Add vegetable mixture, fold, seal edges, and brush with egg wash.

6. Bake until golden.

7. Rest and slice.

8. Serve with fresh herbs and balsamic glaze.

The Digital Age (1990s)

Myron Mixon Inspired:
Peach Bourbon Glazed Pork Butt

In the 1990s, Myron Mixon emerged as a formidable figure in the world of barbecue, revolutionizing traditional techniques with his unmatched expertise. This original Peach Bourbon Glazed Pork Butt recipe pays tribute to Mixon's influence by combining classic smoking methods with innovative flavors. The meticulously crafted rub, featuring smoked paprika, brown sugar, and a blend of spices, exemplifies Mixon's commitment to perfection. The glaze, marrying the sweetness of peach preserves with the boldness of bourbon, reflects Mixon's signature flavor profiles. Slow-smoking the pork butt until fork-tender and basting it with the luscious glaze during the final hour results in a masterpiece that captures Mixon's dedication to elevating barbecue to an art form. This dish not only embodies the essence of Mixon's 1990s barbecue legacy but also stands as a testament to his enduring impact on the world of smoked culinary delights.

Ingredients

For the Pork Butt:
- 1 pork butt (about 6-8 lbs)
- 2 tablespoons smoked paprika
- 2 tablespoons brown sugar
- 1 tablespoon salt
- 1 tablespoon black pepper
- 1 teaspoon garlic powder
- 1 teaspoon onion powder

For the Peach Bourbon Glaze:
- 1 cup peach preserves
- 1/2 cup bourbon
- 1/4 cup apple cider vinegar
- 3 tablespoons Dijon mustard
- 2 tablespoons soy sauce
- 2 cloves garlic, minced
- 1 teaspoon grated fresh ginger
- Salt and black pepper to taste

Instructions

1. Rub pork butt with smoked paprika, brown sugar, salt, pepper, garlic, and onion powder. Marinate.

2. Smoke at 225°F until internal temp reaches 195-205°F.

3. In a saucepan, simmer peach preserves, bourbon, apple cider vinegar, Dijon mustard, soy sauce, garlic, and ginger for the glaze.

4. Brush glaze on the pork during the last hour of smoking.

5. Rest for 30 mins.

6. Slice or shred.

7. Serve with additional glaze.

The Digital Age (1990s)

Martha Stewart Inspired:
Blue Cheese and Walnut Stuffed Grilled Portobellos

In the 1990s, Martha Stewart became synonymous with sophisticated homemaking and culinary finesse. Her influence permeated American households, redefining the standards for elegant yet approachable cuisine. The Martha Stewart of the '90s epitomized a dedication to quality ingredients and a passion for transforming everyday meals into culinary art.

Inspired by Stewart's timeless aesthetic, the Blue Cheese and Walnut Stuffed Grilled Portobellos pay homage to her refined taste. This dish melds the earthy richness of Portobello mushrooms with the luxurious creaminess of Gorgonzola Dolce, echoing Stewart's penchant for balancing flavors. The addition of toasted walnuts and a drizzle of honey elevates the dish to gourmet heights, embodying the essence of Stewart's culinary legacy – a harmonious blend of simplicity, sophistication, and a touch of indulgence.

Ingredients

- 4 large Portobello mushrooms, cleaned and stems removed
- 2 tablespoons extra virgin olive oil
- Salt and freshly ground black pepper

For the Filling:
- 1 cup crumbled Gorgonzola Dolce cheese
- 1/2 cup toasted and chopped walnuts
- 2 tablespoons finely chopped fresh chives
- 1 tablespoon honey
- 1 tablespoon aged balsamic vinegar
- Freshly ground black pepper, to taste

Instructions

1. Brush Portobellos with olive oil, season.

2. Mix Gorgonzola Dolce, toasted walnuts, chives, honey, and aged balsamic.

3. Fill mushrooms generously with the mixture.

4. Grill for 8-10 mins until tender and cheese is golden.

5. Drizzle with aged balsamic and honey.

6. Garnish with chives.

The Digital Age (1990s)

Asian Fusion Blackberry Salad with Sesame-Crusted Goat Cheese

In a deliberate departure from the commonplace and overused raspberry *coulis* and vinaigrettes that saturated '90s culinary trends, this Asian Fusion Blackberry Salad introduces an innovative flavor profile. Rejecting the ordinary, the salad showcases the robust essence of blackberries combined with the exotic notes of galangal in the vinaigrette, delivering a striking departure from the ubiquitous raspberry-laden dishes of the past.

The sesame-crusted goat cheese provides a delightful textural contrast, elevating the dish beyond the predictable. Embracing the so-sought-after uniqueness of the 90s, this salad defies the conventional with its fusion of vibrant ingredients, making it a refreshing departure from the neverending story of raspberry that overtook the 90s pseudo-haute cuisine. It stands as a testament to a palate that craves originality and refuses to succumb to the mundane trends of yesteryears.

Ingredients

For the Salad:
- 6 cups mixed salad greens
- 1 ripe mango, sliced
- 1 cup sesame-crusted goat cheese
- 1 cup fresh blackberries

For the Sesame-Crusted Goat Cheese:
- 1/2 cup sesame seeds
- 200g goat cheese, chilled and cut into rounds
- 2 tablespoons all-purpose flour
- 1 egg, beaten
- Vegetable oil for frying

For the Galangal-Blackberry Vinaigrette:
- 1/4 cup fresh blackberries
- 1 tablespoon grated galangal
- 2 tablespoons rice vinegar
- 1 tablespoon soy sauce
- 3 tablespoons sesame oil
- Salt and pepper to taste

Instructions

1. Toss mixed greens, sliced mango, and fresh blackberries.

2. Coat goat cheese rounds in flour, egg, and sesame seeds.

3. Fry until golden - approximately 2 minutes per side in oil heated to 350°F (175°C). Drain.

4. Add sesame-crusted goat cheese rounds to the bed of fruit and greens.

5. Drizzle with galangal-blackberry vinaigrette.

6. Serve immediately.

The New Millennium (2000s)

Red Rock Bar & Eatery Inspired:
Lobster Dumpling

The Lobster Dumpling, inspired by the culinary spirit of West Hollywood's iconic Sunset Boulevard in the 2000s, encapsulates the vibrant and eclectic food scene of the era. Nestled in the heart of this dynamic locale, the dumpling mirrors the neighborhood's glamorous yet laid-back atmosphere, where culinary innovation thrived. Filled with succulent lobster, a symbol of sophistication, and infused with clear Asian Fusion Dip, it marries diverse flavors reflective of West Hollywood's cosmopolitan influences.

As a representative dish, the Lobster Dumpling pays homage to the fusion cuisine that defined Sunset Boulevard's culinary landscape. It embodies the creativity and boldness characteristic of the 2000s, aligning seamlessly with the spirit of West Hollywood's dining experiences—an amalgamation of glamour, diversity, and a constant pursuit of culinary excellence that made Sunset Boulevard a culinary destination during this vibrant period.

Ingredients

For the Lobster Dumplings:
- 1 lb cooked lobster meat, chopped
- 1/2 cup water chestnuts, finely chopped
- 2 green onions, finely chopped
- 1 tablespoon ginger, minced
- 1 tablespoon soy sauce
- 1 tablespoon sesame oil
- 1 teaspoon sugar
- Round dumpling wrappers
- Cooking spray

For the Clear Asian Fusion Dip:
- 1/4 cup rice vinegar
- 2 tablespoons soy sauce
- 1 tablespoon honey
- 1 teaspoon sesame oil
- 1 teaspoon ginger, grated
- 1 teaspoon garlic, minced
- 1 teaspoon green onions, finely chopped

Instructions

1. Mix lobster, water chestnuts, green onions, ginger, soy sauce, and sesame oil.

2. Fill dumpling wrappers, seal.

3. Lightly coat the steamer basket or parchment paper with cooking spray to create a non-stick surface and steam for approximately 10-12 minutes or until the dumpling wrappers are cooked through. Ensure that the lobster filling is heated and the wrappers become translucent.

Sesame-Ginger Dip:
1. Whisk rice vinegar, soy sauce, honey, sesame oil, ginger, garlic, and green onions.

The New Millennium (2000s)

Smoked Salmon and Cream Cheese Avocado Toast

Avocado toast's modern popularity surged in the 2000s as a symbol of the global culinary shift towards healthier, Instagram-worthy dishes. While the pairing of avocados and bread dates back centuries, the 2000s saw a cultural renaissance in food trends, marked by increased interest in nutritious, visually appealing options. Avocado toast became a staple in trendy cafes and brunch spots, especially in cities like Melbourne and Los Angeles, epitomizing a fusion of taste and health consciousness. Social media platforms, particularly Instagram, played a pivotal role in disseminating images of this aesthetically pleasing dish, turning it into a ubiquitous breakfast choice. The 2000s witnessed avocado toast not just as a nutritious meal but also as a lifestyle statement, influencing culinary landscapes and consumer preferences worldwide. Here, our version pairs the creamy avocado perfectly with the rich, smoky flavor of salmon and the luscious creaminess of cream cheese, creating a luxurious and satisfying morning treat.

Ingredients

- 1 ripe avocado
- 2 slices of whole-grain or your preferred bread, toasted
- 2 tablespoons cream cheese
- Smoked salmon slices
- Capers, for garnish
- Shallots, thinly sliced
- Fresh dill, for garnish
- Lemon wedges, for serving
- Salt and pepper to taste

Instructions

1. Mash a ripe avocado and season with salt and pepper.

2. Toast whole-grain bread to your liking.

3. Spread cream cheese generously on each slice.

4. Layer with the mashed avocado.

5. Arrange smoked salmon on top.

6. Sprinkle capers and add thinly sliced shallots.

7. Garnish with fresh dill.

8. Serve the toast with lemon wedges on the side.

The New Millennium (2000s)

Korean BBQ Tacos

Korean BBQ tacos emerged as a delicious fusion of Korean and Mexican cuisines, gaining popularity in the early 2000s. This culinary innovation reflects the diversity and creativity in the modern food landscape. The concept often involves marinating beef, pork, or chicken in classic Korean barbecue flavors like soy, garlic, and sesame, then grilling the meat to perfection. The grilled protein is typically served in a taco, accompanied by traditional Korean condiments such as kimchi, ssamjang (a spicy paste), and pickled vegetables. This blending of bold Korean flavors with the handheld convenience of Mexican tacos became a hit, especially in food trucks and trendy eateries. Korean BBQ tacos showcase the cross-cultural culinary exchange that defines contemporary food trends, appealing to a wide audience with its harmonious blend of savory, spicy, and umami flavors.

Ingredients

For the Marinade:
- 1 pound thinly sliced beef (ribeye or flank steak)
- 1/4 cup soy sauce
- 2 tablespoons brown sugar
- 2 tablespoons rice vinegar
- 1 tablespoon sesame oil
- 3 cloves garlic, minced
- 1 teaspoon grated ginger
- 1 tablespoon *mirin* (optional)
- 1 tablespoon *gochujang* (Korean red pepper paste, optional for spice)

For the Tacos:
- 8 small flour or corn tortillas
- Kimchi (store-bought or homemade)
- Sliced green onions
- Sesame seeds (optional)
- Fresh cilantro, chopped (optional)
- Lime wedges

Instructions

1. Marinate thinly sliced beef in soy sauce, brown sugar, rice vinegar, sesame oil, minced garlic, grated ginger, and mirin/gochujang (optional). Refrigerate for 30 mins or more.

2. Grill marinated beef for 2-3 mins per side.

3. Warm tortillas.

4. Assemble tacos with grilled beef, kimchi, sliced green onions, sesame seeds, and cilantro.

5. Serve with lime wedges.

The New Millennium (2000s)

Lemon Vermicelli with Roasted Garlic and Asiago

The Lemon Vermicelli with Roasted Garlic and Asiago encapsulates quintessentially American and 2000s culinary trends with a harmonious blend of global influences. Roasting garlic, a technique embraced in American kitchens, imparts a rich, caramelized depth to the dish, elevating the vermicelli with a comforting aroma. The use of Asiago cheese, reflecting a growing interest in artisanal and specialty cheeses during the 2000s, adds a nuanced sharpness. The lemony zing, a nod to fresh, vibrant flavors, embodies the era's shift towards lighter, healthier cuisine. This recipe fuses American preferences for robust, savory profiles with a contemporary inclination for sophisticated, yet accessible, global-inspired dishes—a perfect embodiment of culinary trends that marked American kitchens in the 2000s.

Ingredients

8 oz (225g) vermicelli noodles
1 head of garlic
1/4 cup olive oil
Zest and juice of 2 lemons
Salt and black pepper to taste
1 cup shaved Asiago cheese
Fresh parsley, chopped, for garnish

Instructions

1. Preheat the oven to 400°F (200°C).

2. Cut off the top of the garlic head to expose the cloves.

3. Drizzle the garlic head with olive oil, wrap it in foil, and roast in the oven for 30-40 minutes until the cloves are soft and golden.

4. Cook the vermicelli according to package instructions, then drain and set aside.

5. Squeeze the roasted garlic cloves into a bowl, add olive oil, lemon zest, lemon juice, salt, and black pepper. Mix into a smooth sauce.

6. Toss the cooked vermicelli in the roasted garlic sauce until well coated.

7. Serve the lemony vermicelli in bowls, topped with generous shavings of Asiago cheese.

8. Garnish with chopped fresh parsley and additional black pepper if desired.

The New Millennium (2000s)

Lemon Vermicelli with Quick Pickled Vegetables and Pecorino

In the 2000s, the inclusion of Lemon Vermicelli recipes with diverse flavor profiles reflects the era's culinary landscape, marked by a fusion of global influences and an increased focus on fresh, vibrant ingredients. The Lemon Vermicelli with Roasted Garlic and Asiago embodies the era's appreciation for comforting, savory richness. The roasted garlic, an American kitchen staple, adds depth, while Asiago reflects the rising interest in specialty cheeses. Conversely, the Lemon Vermicelli with Quick Pickled Vegetables and Pecorino represents a lighter, more tangy side of 2000s cuisine. Quick pickling, inspired by global tastes, enhances the dish with a refreshing twist, and Pecorino showcases the era's enthusiasm for diverse and artisanal cheese options. Together, these recipes exemplify the culinary crossroads of indulgence and freshness that defined American food in the 2000s.

Ingredients

8 oz (225g) vermicelli noodles
1 cup thinly sliced cucumbers
1 cup thinly sliced radishes
1/2 cup rice vinegar
2 tablespoons sugar
Zest and juice of 2 lemons
Salt to taste
1 cup shaved Pecorino cheese
Fresh cilantro, chopped, for garnish

Instructions

1. Cook the vermicelli according to package instructions, then drain and set aside.

2. In a bowl, combine sliced cucumbers and radishes.

3. In a small saucepan, heat rice vinegar and sugar until the sugar dissolves. Pour the mixture over the sliced vegetables.

4. Add lemon zest, lemon juice, and salt to the pickling mixture. Toss well and let it sit for about 15-20 minutes.

5. Drain the pickled vegetables, reserving some of the pickling liquid.

6. Toss the cooked vermicelli with the pickled vegetables and a few tablespoons of the pickling liquid.

7. Serve the lemony vermicelli in bowls, topped with generous shavings of Pecorino cheese.

8. Garnish with chopped fresh cilantro and additional salt if needed.

The New Millennium (2000s)

Caribbean Jerk Shrimp and Mango Salsa Bowl

The Caribbean Jerk Shrimp and Mango Salsa Bowl epitomizes the culinary zeitgeist of the 2000s. In an era marked by a fervent embrace of flavor fusion, this dish boldly marries the robust kick of Caribbean jerk seasoning with the luscious sweetness of mango salsa. Reflecting a newfound fascination with global tastes, it draws inspiration from Caribbean cuisine, infusing a vibrant tapestry of spices and ingredients into mainstream dining. As the decade encouraged an adventurous culinary spirit, the bowl's spicy and refreshing amalgamation perfectly aligns with the era's penchant for bold flavors. With the rise of food media and a growing emphasis on fresh, colorful ingredients, this dish stands as a testament to the 2000s' dynamic and eclectic approach to gastronomy.

Ingredients

- 1 lb large shrimp, peeled and deveined
- 2 tablespoons Caribbean jerk seasoning
- 2 tablespoons olive oil
- 2 cups cooked jasmine rice
- 1 ripe mango, diced
- 1/2 red onion, finely chopped
- 1 red bell pepper, diced
- 1 jalapeño, seeded and minced
- Juice of 2 limes
- Fresh cilantro, chopped, for garnish
- 3 green onions, chopped
Salt and pepper to taste

Instructions

1. In a bowl, toss shrimp with Caribbean jerk seasoning, ensuring each shrimp is well coated.

2. Heat olive oil in a skillet over medium-high heat. Add the seasoned shrimp and cook for 2-3 minutes per side or until opaque and slightly charred. Set aside.

3. In a large bowl, combine diced mango, green onion, red bell pepper, jalapeño, lime juice, salt, and pepper. Mix well to create the mango salsa.

4. Assemble the bowl by placing a serving of cooked jasmine rice at the base.

5. Top the rice with the jerk-seasoned shrimp.

6. Spoon generous amounts of mango salsa over the shrimp, and garnish with fresh cilantro, and serve immediately

The New Millennium (2000s)

Lemongrass Infused Pad See Ew with Rapini and Shrimp

The 2000s marked a significant rise in the popularity of Thai cuisine in the United States, as diners sought diverse and exotic flavors. Thai food became a culinary trend, celebrated for its bold combinations of sweet, sour, salty, and spicy elements. Our Lemongrass Infused Pad See Ew with Rapini and Shrimp is an ode to the 2000s culinary scene, encapsulating the era's love for diverse global flavors and innovative ingredient pairings. Originally conceived as featuring the mild sweetness of Broccolini, this adaptation introduces Rapini's distinct bitterness. The lemongrass-infused sauce intertwines with Rapini's peppery notes, creating a harmonious blend. The tender-crisp texture of Rapini harmonizes with succulent shrimp, providing a contemporary twist on the classic. Reflecting the 2000s spirit, this rendition embraces dynamic fusion, showcasing the era's affinity for unique tastes and ongoing exploration of fresh, vibrant ingredients.

Ingredients

- 8 oz wide rice noodles
- 1 lb large shrimp, peeled and deveined
- 1 bunch rapini
- 2 tablespoons vegetable oil
- 3 cloves garlic, minced
- 2 tablespoons soy sauce
- 2 tablespoons oyster sauce
- 1 tablespoon fish sauce
- 1 tablespoon sugar
- 1 stalk lemongrass, bruised and cut into 2-inch pieces
- 1 cup bean sprouts
- Fresh cilantro leaves for garnish
- Lime wedges for serving

Instructions

1. Cook wide rice noodles; set aside.

2. Simmer lemongrass in coconut milk for flavor; strain and set aside.

3. Sauté minced garlic in vegetable oil until fragrant.

4. Cook shrimp until pink; set aside.

5. In the same pan, stir-fry rapini until tender.

6. Add cooked noodles, soy sauce, oyster sauce, fish sauce, and sugar to the pan.

7. Pour in lemongrass-infused liquid; stir-fry until coated.

8. Return shrimp to the pan; toss with noodles and rapini.

9. Add bean sprouts; toss briefly.

10. Remove lemongrass pieces.

11. Serve hot, garnished with cilantro and lime wedges.

The Social Media Era (2010s)

Pumpkin & Sage Cauliflower Crust Pizza

The cauliflower crust pizza trend in the 2010s gained traction with the growing popularity of low-carb and gluten-free diets. While it's challenging to attribute the creation of cauliflower crust pizza to a single individual, food bloggers and chefs played a significant role in popularizing the idea. Early recipes and experiments started circulating online, with individuals sharing their experiences of using cauliflower as a pizza crust alternative.

Cauliflower crust pizza's appeal lies in its versatility. Toppings and combinations can vary widely, but popular choices include classic Margherita, vegetable-loaded, or even more exotic options like BBQ chicken or buffalo cauliflower. The crust's neutral flavor allows it to complement various toppings, and it provides a satisfying, crunchy texture when baked properly. The trend reflects a broader shift in the 2010s towards exploring alternative ingredients and healthier adaptations of traditional dishes.

Ingredients

For the Cauliflower Crust:
- 1 medium-sized cauliflower, riced (about 3 cups)
- 1 egg
- 1 cup shredded mozzarella cheese
- 1 teaspoon dried oregano
- 1/2 teaspoon garlic powder
- Salt and pepper to taste

For the Toppings:
- 1/2 cup pumpkin puree
- 1/2 cup shredded mozzarella cheese
- Fresh sage leaves
- 1/4 cup caramelized onions
- 1/4 cup crumbled goat cheese
- 1/4 cup chopped walnuts
- Salt and pepper to taste

Instructions

1. Mix riced cauliflower with egg, mozzarella, oregano, and garlic to create the cauliflower crust.

2. Press the cauliflower mixture onto a baking sheet.

3. Bake the cauliflower crust until it sets.

4. Top the crust with pumpkin puree, mozzarella, caramelized onions, goat cheese, walnuts, and fresh sage.

5. Bake the pizza until the cheese melts.

6. Garnish the finished pizza with fresh sage.

7. Slice and savor your delightful Pumpkin Sage Cauliflower Crust Pizza!

The Social Media Era (2010s)

Ramen Burger

In the culinary landscape of the 2010s, the ramen burger emerged as a trendsetting fusion dish, blending the beloved Japanese noodle soup with the iconic American burger. The brainchild of chef Keizo Shimamoto, the ramen burger made its debut at a Brooklyn food market in 2013, instantly capturing the attention of food enthusiasts and media alike. The innovative creation replaced traditional buns with compact patties made of ramen noodles bound together with egg and grilled until crispy. The dish gained viral popularity, with long lines forming at food festivals and pop-up events. The ramen burger symbolized a cultural crossroads, blending Eastern and Western flavors in a handheld, Instagram-worthy package. While its fame waned, the ramen burger left a lasting imprint on culinary experimentation, showcasing the power of cross-cultural gastronomy in defining food trends during the vibrant 2010s.

Ingredients

For the Kimchi Pork Patty:
- 1 pound ground pork
- 1 cup kimchi, finely chopped
- 2 green onions, finely chopped
- 2 tablespoons soy sauce
- 1 tablespoon sesame oil
- 1 tablespoon *gochugaru* (Korean red pepper flakes, adjust to taste)
- Salt and pepper to taste

For the Ramen Bun:
- 2 packs of instant ramen noodles
- 2 large eggs, beaten
- Cooking oil for frying

For Assembly:
- *Gochujang* mayo (mix *gochujang* with mayonnaise)
- Pickled radishes
- Lettuce leaves

Instructions

1. Combine ground pork with finely chopped kimchi, green onions, soy sauce, sesame oil, gochugaru, salt, and pepper to make the Kimchi Pork mixture.

2. Shape the mixture into patties and cook until fully done.

3. Cook ramen noodles, mix with beaten eggs, shape into patties, and fry until golden brown for the unique bun.

4. Spread gochujang mayo on the ramen buns.

5. Place a kimchi pork patty on the bottom bun.

6. Add pickled radishes and lettuce.

7. Top with another ramen bun!

The Social Media Era (2010s)

Reverse Seared Steak

The Reverse Sear Steak represents an accessible entry into the realm of molecular gastronomy for home cooks, offering a culinary adventure without requiring specialized equipment or elusive chemicals. In the spirit of contemporary cuisine prevalent in the 2010s, this method showcases precision cooking. The low-temperature oven roast achieves a uniformly cooked interior, while the subsequent hot pan sear crafts a delectably caramelized crust. Embracing the principles of molecular gastronomy, the reverse sear elevates the home-cooked steak experience without the need for a siphon whip or esoteric ingredients. It exemplifies a fusion of scientific precision and traditional culinary techniques, making the avant-garde approach to cooking accessible to all, and serves as a perfect culmination to the diverse and innovative culinary landscape of the past decade.

Ingredients

- Thick-cut steak (ribeye, New York strip, or filet mignon)
- Salt and pepper
- Olive oil or clarified butter

Instructions

1. Preheat the oven to 225°F (107°C).

2. Season the steak with salt and pepper.

3. Roast the steak on a wire rack until it reaches 10-15°F below the desired doneness.

4. Allow the steak to rest for 10-15 minutes.

5. Preheat a skillet with olive oil or clarified butter.

6. Sear the steak for 1-2 minutes per side until a golden crust forms.

7. Let the steak rest again for a few minutes.

8. Slice the steak against the grain and serve.

The Atomized Era (2020s)

Sakura Blossom Sushi Rice Pudding

Transport yourself to the enchanting world of Japanese culinary artistry with our Sakura Blossom Sushi Rice Pudding. Inspired by the delicate beauty of sakura blossoms, this recipe harmoniously blends tradition and modernity, creating a delightful dessert suitable for the 2020s in the U.S.

In this fusion, we take the allure of sushi rice and infuse it with a luscious blend of whole milk, sugar, vanilla, and the subtle essence of sakura blossom syrup. The result is a creamy and indulgent pudding that captures the essence of springtime in Japan. The infusion process not only imparts a unique floral flavor but also pays homage to the age-old tradition of appreciating sakura blossoms. Garnished with sakura blossoms, this pudding is a sensory journey, inviting you to savor the delicate elegance of Japanese culinary heritage in the contemporary American kitchen.

Ingredients

- 1 cup sushi rice
- 2 1/2 cups whole milk
- 1/2 cup sugar
- 1/2 teaspoon salt
- 1 teaspoon vanilla extract
- 1 tablespoon *sakura* blossom syrup (can be found in Japanese or specialty stores)
- *Sakura* blossoms (dried or fresh, for garnish)

Homemade Cherry Blossom Syrup (the sakura syrup alternative):
1 cup water, 1 cup granulated sugar, 1-2 teaspoons cherry blossom extract (available online or at specialty baking stores) Combine 1 cup water, 1 cup sugar. Heat until dissolved. Add 1-2 tsp cherry blossom extract. Simmer 10 mins. Strain, cool.

If cherry blossom extract is unavailable, an easy alternative is using almond extract. It provides a delightful, subtle nutty flavor, complementing the sweetness of the syrup. Start with 1/2 teaspoon, adjusting to taste.

Instructions

1. Rinse and cook 1 cup of sushi rice.

2. In a separate pot, simmer 2 1/2 cups of milk, 1/2 cup of sugar, and a pinch of salt.

3. Add 1 teaspoon of vanilla and 1 tablespoon of sakura syrup to the milk mixture.

4. Infuse the mixture for 10-15 minutes, then strain it.

5. Mix the cooked rice with the sakura-infused milk.

6. Continue cooking until the mixture thickens.

7. Chill the prepared rice and milk mixture.

8. Garnish with sakura blossoms before serving.

The Atomized Era (2020s)

Aji Amarillo Massaman Curry Beef

Our Aji Amarillo Massaman Curry Beef recipe mirrors the rich tapestry of American culinary culture, embodying a fusion of diverse influences. Rooted in the Peruvian tradition with the inclusion of Aji Amarillo paste, this dish elegantly merges with Thai Massaman curry, showcasing the global interconnectedness of contemporary American households. The history behind this dish is a journey through flavors, tracing the pathways of cultural exchange and adaptation. It symbolizes the American family's openness to embracing and celebrating the amalgamation of varied culinary heritages. As families explore global tastes in their kitchens, this recipe stands as a testament to the evolving and inclusive nature of American cuisine, reflecting the interconnected narratives of people and flavors across borders and generations.

Ingredients

- 1.5 lbs (700g) beef stew meat, cubed
- 2 tablespoons vegetable oil
- 2 tablespoons Aji Amarillo paste
- 2 tablespoons Massaman curry paste
- 1 can (14 oz) coconut milk
- 1 large onion, sliced
- 3 cloves garlic, minced
- 1 tablespoon grated ginger
- 2 tablespoons Massaman curry powder
- 2 tablespoons tamarind paste
- 2 tablespoons brown sugar
- 1 cinnamon stick
- 3 cardamom pods
- 3 whole cloves
- 1 cup beef or vegetable broth
- 2 large potatoes, peeled and diced
- 1/2 cup roasted peanuts (optional)
- Fresh cilantro for garnish
- Cooked jasmine rice for serving

Instructions

1. Brown beef cubes in vegetable oil, then set aside.
2. Sauté sliced onions, minced garlic, and grated ginger in the same pot.
3. Stir in Aji Amarillo paste and Massaman curry paste, cook briefly.
4. Add coconut milk, broth, browned beef, Massaman curry powder, tamarind paste, and brown sugar. Add cinnamon stick, cardamom pods, and whole cloves.
5. Simmer covered for 1.5-2 hours until beef is tender. Add diced potatoes in the last 30 minutes.
6. Adjust seasoning, remove cinnamon stick, cardamom pods, and cloves.
7. Serve over jasmine rice, garnish with peanuts (optional) and cilantro.

The Atomized Era (2020s)

Meyer Lemon Pork and Grape Skewer Tapas

This Meyer Lemon Pork and Grape Skewer Tapas seamlessly blend Mediterranean and Spanish influences, creating a harmonious fusion of flavors. The Meyer lemon marinade, with its delicate sweetness and citrusy zing, pays homage to Mediterranean cuisine, while the grilled pork and grapes nod to the Spanish tradition of combining savory and sweet elements. The result is a tapas dish that balances the richness of marinated pork with the burst of sweetness from the grapes, all elevated by the aromatic infusion of Meyer lemon and rosemary. When tasted, each tapa delivers a succulent bite, where the tender pork complements the juicy, caramelized grapes. Pair this dish with a crisp Spanish white wine or a refreshing sangria to accentuate the citrus undertones, creating a delightful and refreshing tapas experience.

Ingredients

For the Meyer Lemon Marinade:
- 1/3 cup extra-virgin olive oil
- 1/4 cup Meyer lemon juice (about 2-3 Meyer lemons)
- 2 tablespoons honey
- 2 cloves garlic, minced
- 1 teaspoon Dijon mustard
- 1 tablespoon fresh rosemary, finely chopped
- Salt and black pepper to taste

For the Pork and Grape Skewers:
- 1 1/2 pounds pork tenderloin, cut into tapas-sized cubes
- 2 cups red seedless grapes, washed and stemmed
- Wooden skewers, soaked in water for at least 30 minutes

Instructions

1. Combine olive oil, Meyer lemon juice, honey, minced garlic, Dijon mustard, chopped rosemary, salt, and pepper.

2. Cut pork tenderloin into cubes.

3. Wash grapes and soak wooden skewers.

4. Marinate pork in the lemon mixture for 1-2 hours.

5. Preheat the grill.

6. Thread pork and grapes onto skewers.

7. Grill for 10-12 minutes, turning occasionally.

8. Let skewers rest.

9. Serve hot, garnished with rosemary.

The Atomized Era (2020s)

Slow-Cooked Freekeh and Chicken Casserole

The Slow-Cooked Freekeh and Chicken Casserole, deeply rooted in Arabic culinary heritage, draws inspiration from traditional Levantine dishes. Freekeh, roasted green wheat, reflects a centuries-old Middle Eastern cooking tradition, celebrated for its nutty flavor and nutritional richness. The marriage of aromatic spices, succulent chicken, and wholesome freekeh epitomizes the essence of Arabic comfort food.

Freekeh is roasted green wheat, offering a nutty flavor and nutritional benefits. You can find freekeh in well-stocked grocery stores, health food stores, or online retailers.

For a readily available alternative, opt for bulgur, made from cracked wheat with a mild, nutty flavor, and its quick cooking time makes it a convenient substitute for freekeh in this recipe.

Ingredients

- 1 cup freekeh, rinsed
- 4 bone-in, skin-on chicken thighs
- 1 large onion, finely chopped
- 3 carrots, sliced
- 3 celery stalks, chopped
- 4 cloves garlic, minced
- 1 teaspoon ground cumin
- 1 teaspoon ground coriander
- 1 teaspoon smoked paprika
- 1/2 teaspoon turmeric
- Salt and black pepper to taste
- 4 cups chicken broth
- 1 can (15 oz) chickpeas, drained and rinsed
- 1 cup frozen peas
- Fresh parsley, chopped (for garnish)

Instructions

1. Sear chicken thighs.
2. Place seared chicken in a slow cooker.
3. Add freekeh, chopped onion, carrots, celery, minced garlic, cumin, coriander, smoked paprika, turmeric, salt, and pepper.
4. Pour chicken broth over the ingredients.
5. Cook on low for 6-8 hours.
6. Add chickpeas and peas in the last 30 minutes of cooking.
7. Shred the cooked chicken.
8. Stir the shredded chicken back into the casserole.
9. Garnish with fresh parsley.
10. Enjoy!

The Atomized Era (2020s)

Herb-Infused Adobo Chicken Burrito

Adobo chicken, a staple in Filipino cuisine, traces its roots to Spanish colonization. The technique involves slow-cooking meat in a soy-vinegar blend, embodying a harmonious blend of indigenous and foreign flavors. In the United States, a cultural melting pot, *adobo* chicken has evolved, becoming a symbol of diversity and culinary innovation. This Herb-Infused *Adobo* Chicken Burrito, a fusion of Filipino *adobo* with Mexican burrito elements, encapsulates the inclusive spirit of the United States in 2024. It mirrors a nation that embraces diversity, celebrating its cultural tapestry through food. As American cuisine continues to evolve, this fusion recipe signifies a perfect expression of the dynamic culinary landscape, where different traditions blend seamlessly to create a harmonious and flavorful reflection of the nation's diverse heritage.

Ingredients

For the Herb-Infused Adobo Chicken:
- 2 pounds chicken, cut into pieces
- 1 cup soy sauce
- 1 cup vinegar
- 1 cup coconut milk
- 1/2 cup brown sugar
- 1 head garlic, minced
- 1 tablespoon peppercorns
- 3 bay leaves
- Fresh herbs (thyme or rosemary), a handful, finely chopped

For the Burrito:
- Large flour tortillas
- Cooked white rice
- Black beans, drained and rinsed
- Shredded lettuce
- Diced tomatoes
- Grated cheddar cheese
- Fresh cilantro, chopped
- Sour cream (optional)

Instructions

1. Marinate chicken in soy sauce, vinegar, coconut milk, garlic, herbs for 1-2 hours.

2. Cook until tender.

3. Fill tortillas with rice, beans, adobo chicken, lettuce, tomatoes, cheese.

4. Roll tightly.

5. Serve with cilantro and optional sour cream.

6. Enjoy the fusion of Filipino adobo and Mexican burrito flavors!

The Atomized Era (2020s)

Plum and Almond Brownie Bars with Boozy Twist

This Plum & Almond Boozy Brownie Bars recipe beautifully marries flavors, symbolizing the 2020s' culinary spirit. Plums, cherished in culinary history, bring a sweet and tart profile to various global cuisines. Their use dates back centuries, from traditional European desserts to Middle Eastern stews. This recipe, fusing the richness of chocolate and almonds with the fruity essence of plums, encapsulates the modern era's penchant for cultural fusion. As the 2020s embraced diverse influences, this mash-up reflects a global culinary consciousness, where ingredients harmonize across borders. The addition of a boozy twist infuses a contemporary touch, echoing the decade's adventurous and innovative gastronomic landscape. These brownie bars, marrying tradition with innovation, exemplify the evolving palate of a culinary world ready for boundary-breaking creations in the 2020s.

Ingredients

For the Brownie Bars:
- 1 cup unsalted butter, melted
- 2 cups granulated sugar
- 4 large eggs
- 1 teaspoon almond extract
- 1 cup all-purpose flour
- 1/2 cup cocoa powder
- 1/4 teaspoon salt
- 1 cup fresh plums, finely chopped

For the Plum Glaze:
- 1/2 cup plum jam or puree
- 2 tablespoons brandy or Amaretto (adjust to taste)

Instructions

1. Mix melted butter, sugar, eggs, almond extract, flour, cocoa, salt.

2. Fold in chopped plums.

3. Bake at 350°F for 25-30 mins.

4. Simmer plum jam with brandy.

5. Brush over cooled brownies.

6. Chill, slice, and optionally drizzle with more brandy.

7. Indulge in this rich, fruity, and boozy delight!

The Atomized Era (2020s)

Chocolate-Coconut Stout Barley Pudding

The Chocolate-Coconut Stout Barley Pudding encapsulates the spirit of culinary evolution in 2020s U.S. kitchens, seamlessly merging tradition with innovation. Combining the wholesome charm of barley with the bold richness of stout beer, this dessert represents a convergence of generational approaches to cooking. As families pass down time-honored recipes, the addition of stout infuses a contemporary twist, showcasing a willingness to experiment and adapt. The pudding's velvety texture and harmonious blend of chocolate and coconut pay homage to classic flavors, while the inclusion of stout beer introduces a modern and unexpected element. It mirrors the diverse influences shaping American kitchens, symbolizing a collective effort to bridge culinary traditions with a progressive embrace of new ingredients, epitomizing the dynamic and inclusive nature of 2020s American gastronomy.

Ingredients

- 1 cup pearl barley
- 2 1/2 cups coconut milk
- 1 cup stout beer (choose a chocolate or oatmeal stout for enhanced flavor)
- 1/3 cup cocoa powder
- 1/2 cup sugar (adjust to taste)
- Pinch of salt
- 1 teaspoon vanilla extract

Instructions

1. Rinse the pearl barley under cold water.

2. In the slow-cooker, combine barley, coconut milk, stout beer, cocoa powder, sugar, and a pinch of salt.

3. Stir well to ensure the cocoa powder is fully incorporated.

4. Cook on low for 6-8 hours or until the barley is tender and the pudding has thickened.

6. Stir in vanilla extract during the last 15 minutes of cooking.

7. Adjust sugar to taste.

8. Serve warm, either on its own or with a dollop of whipped cream or a scoop of vanilla ice cream.

The Atomized Era (2020s)

Bourbon Pecan Apple Butter

Traditional apple butter, rooted in colonial America, combined apples, sugar, and spices, slow-cooked to a velvety spread. In the 2020s, a culinary evolution embraces the avant-garde. Enter Bourbon Pecan Apple Butter, a modern twist on this classic. A harmonious dance of apples, brown sugar, and cinnamon meets the bold embrace of bourbon, complemented by toasted pecans for a delightful crunch. This contemporary rendition adds a layer of complexity, appealing to the sophisticated palates of the present era. Crafted with care in a slow cooker, this fusion of flavors elevates the nostalgic essence of traditional apple butter, embodying the spirit of culinary exploration in the 21st century. It's a sensory journey, marrying heritage with innovation, making Bourbon Pecan Apple Butter a delicious hallmark of the culinary landscape in the modern age.

Ingredients

- 8 cups peeled, cored, and chopped apples (a mix of varieties)
- 1 cup brown sugar
- 1 teaspoon ground cinnamon
- 1/2 cup bourbon
- 1 cup chopped toasted pecans

Instructions

1. Peel, core, and chop 8 cups of apples.

2. In a slow cooker, combine apples, 1 cup brown sugar, and 1 teaspoon ground cinnamon.

3. Pour 1/2 cup bourbon over the mixture and stir well.

4. Cook on low for 6-8 hours until apples are tender and the mixture thickens.

5. In the last hour, stir in 1 cup chopped toasted pecans.

6. Use an immersion blender or transfer to a blender for a smooth consistency.

7. Allow the bourbon pecan apple butter to cool.

8. Store in jars in the refrigerator.

9. Spread on toast, mix into yogurt, or enjoy by the spoonful.

The Atomized Era (2020s)

Wine-Soaked Tomato Peach Parfait

Rooted in the culinary wisdom of our historic ancestors, the Wine-Soaked Tomato Peach Parfait embraces a simple tradition and offers a modern twist, making it an ideal indulgence for the sophisticated palates of the 2020s. Drawing inspiration from age-old practices of marinating fruits in wine, this recipe seamlessly melds heritage with contemporary flavors. Tomatoes and peaches, meticulously soaked in a white wine infusion, evoke a delicate balance between sweetness and subtle acidity. The choice of vanilla yogurt introduces a creamy texture, harmonizing the layers into a refreshing parfait. This innovative dessert captures the essence of traditional wine-soaked fruits while embracing the modern demand for unique and sophisticated taste experiences. With a nod to the past and a flair for the present, this parfait stands as a testament to the timeless appeal of culinary innovation, making it a delectable treat for the discerning tastes of the 2020s.

Ingredients

- 2 large tomatoes, diced
- 3 ripe peaches, peeled and diced
- 1 cup white wine (such as Sauvignon Blanc or Pinot Grigio)
- 2 tablespoons honey
- 2 cups vanilla yogurt
- Fresh mint leaves for garnish (optional)

Instructions

1. Dice 2 large tomatoes and 3 ripe, peeled peaches.

2. Combine tomatoes, peaches, 1 cup white wine, and 2 tablespoons honey in a bowl.

3. Refrigerate the mixture for at least 2 hours or overnight to marinate.

4. In serving glasses, layer the wine-soaked tomato and peach mixture with 2 cups vanilla yogurt.

5. Begin with a spoonful of the fruit mixture, followed by a layer of yogurt. Repeat until the glass is filled.

6. Optionally, garnish with fresh mint leaves.

7. Chill the parfaits in the refrigerator for about 30 minutes before serving.

8. Enjoy the harmonious balance of the wine-infused fruit's subtle sweetness and acidity with the creamy vanilla yogurt.

9. Optionally pair with a glass of the same white wine used in the recipe for a complementary tasting experience for a complementary tasting experience.

The Atomized Era (2020s)

Gazpacho Granita

Gazpacho Granita, a delightful fusion of traditional gazpacho and the icy allure of granita, emerges as the perfect savory delight for the culinary landscape of the 2020s. Its inception combines the refreshing essence of ripe tomatoes, crisp cucumber, vibrant bell peppers, and aromatic garlic, creating a harmonious symphony of flavors. The addition of tomato juice, red wine vinegar, and olive oil transforms the mixture into a smooth, invigorating elixir. Seasoned with salt and black pepper, each spoonful offers a burst of freshness and a tantalizing complexity. Gazpacho Granita, with its granular texture achieved through a freezing process, stands out as a versatile option. Whether served as an *amuse-bouche* at the beginning of a meal or as a palate-cleansing finale, this innovative dish encapsulates the essence of contemporary culinary trends—offering a refreshing, savory journey for discerning palates in the evolving gastronomic landscape of the 2020s.

Ingredients

- 4 large ripe tomatoes, chopped
- 1 cucumber, peeled and chopped
- 1 red bell pepper, chopped
- 1 small red onion, chopped
- 2 cloves garlic, minced
- 3 cups tomato juice
- 1/4 cup red wine vinegar
- 1/4 cup olive oil
- 1 teaspoon salt
- 1/2 teaspoon black pepper
- Fresh basil or cilantro for garnish

Instructions

1. Combine tomatoes, cucumber, red bell pepper, red onion, and garlic in a blender until finely chopped.

2. Add tomato juice, red wine vinegar, and olive oil. Blend until smooth.

3. Season with salt and black pepper. Adjust to taste.

4. Optionally strain for a smoother texture.

5. Pour the mixture into a dish and freeze.

6. Every hour, scrape the frozen edges with a fork until granular.

7. Spoon into glasses or bowls.

8. Garnish with fresh basil or cilantro. Serve and enjoy!

The Atomized Era (2020s)

Blue Cheese and Walnut No-Churn Ice Cream

This flavor mash-up reflects the innovative spirit of modern American cuisine. Drawing inspiration from the playfulness of contemporary gastronomy, it pushes boundaries by pairing unexpected ingredients. The tradition of experimenting with sweet and savory combinations has deep roots, but the 2020s see a resurgence of such daring creations, symbolizing a culinary landscape that embraces creativity and surprises the palate with unconventional yet harmonious flavors.

The velvety texture combines with the savory tang of blue cheese and the crunch of chopped walnuts, creating a delightful symphony of flavors. Each bite offers a unique balance between the sweetness of the cream, the boldness of the blue cheese, and the nutty undertones.

Ingredients

- 2 cups heavy cream, chilled
1 can (14 ounces) sweetened condensed milk
4 ounces blue cheese, crumbled
1/2 cup chopped walnuts
1 teaspoon vanilla extract
Pinch of salt

Instructions

1. Whip 2 cups of chilled heavy cream in a large bowl until stiff peaks form.

2. Gently fold in 1 can (14 ounces) sweetened condensed milk and 1 teaspoon vanilla extract until well combined.

3. Add 4 ounces crumbled blue cheese to the mixture and fold it in.

4. Fold in 1/2 cup chopped walnuts.

5. Pour the ice cream mixture into a lidded container or a loaf pan.

6. Cover and freeze for at least 6 hours or overnight.

7. When ready to serve, let the ice cream soften for a few minutes at room temperature.

8. Scoop into bowls or cones, and optionally garnish with additional chopped walnuts.

The Atomized Era (2020s)

Caribbean Spiced Rum Banana Foster Tart

As a sweet finale in this idiosyncratic cookbook celebrating American classics, the Caribbean Spiced Rum Banana Foster Tart stands as a testament to the rich tapestry of culinary influences shaping the nation's gastronomy. This decadent tart melds the warmth of Caribbean spices with the comfort of bananas foster, embodying the fusion that defines American cuisine. A graham cracker crust cradles a luscious filling of caramelized bananas soaked in spiced rum, bringing forth a tropical symphony. Just as American culinary traditions owe their vibrancy to immigrants, industry, and evolving tastes, this tart encapsulates the essence of diverse flavors uniting harmoniously. With warm wishes for your culinary journey, may this dessert be a sweet reminder that, much like this cookbook, America's culinary narrative thrives on innovation, adaptation, and the embrace of varied cultural contributions. Enjoy!

Ingredients

For the Crust:
- 1 1/2 cups graham cracker crumbs
- 1/2 cup melted unsalted butter
- 1/4 cup granulated sugar

For the Banana Foster Filling:
- 4 ripe bananas, sliced
- 1/2 cup unsalted butter
- 1 cup brown sugar
- 1/4 cup Caribbean spiced rum
- 1 teaspoon ground cinnamon
- 1/2 teaspoon nutmeg

For the Whipped Cream Topping:
- 1 cup heavy cream
- 2 tablespoons powdered sugar
- 1 teaspoon vanilla extract

Instructions

Mix graham crumbs, melted butter, and sugar; press into slow cooker. In skillet, melt butter; add bananas, brown sugar, rum, cinnamon, and nutmeg. Cook until caramelized. Spread over crust. Cook on low 2-3 hrs. Whip cream, sugar, and vanilla. Spoon over cooled tart. Chill. Enjoy this tropical delight!

Final Thoughts

In this culinary sojourn across the heart of American classics, I find myself reflecting on the diverse array of recipes that have graced our kitchens. Each dish is a testament to the multifaceted tapestry of flavors that defines the rich, cultural mosaic of American cuisine.

From the coastal allure of Shellfish and Sea Vegetable Three Sisters Stew to the rustic charm of Johnnycakes with Rosemary Brown Butter, and the sweet indulgence of Ash Cake with Berry Compote and Lavender – each recipe weaves a chapter in the historical narrative of American culinary heritage. As I ponder this gastronomic journey, I am reminded of the ever-evolving nature of our culinary landscape.

The refinement of Hoecakes into an elevated version with a Cider Reduction Glaze showcases the adaptability and sophistication inherent in American cooking. The regional nuances in dishes like Clam Chowder with Bacon and Leek or the Smoked Salmon and Cream Cheese Avocado Toast illustrate the dynamic interplay of flavors, a reflection of our nation's diverse cultural influences.

As we draw the curtains on this culinary exploration, I encourage you to immerse yourself in the delightful flavors of the Pacific Northwest Salmon Chowder and savor the crisp textures of Oregon Hazelnut-Crusted Chicken, both capturing the essence of the West. Indulge in the complex notes of Manhattan Clam Chow Mein, the soulful Harlem Renaissance Spiced Sweet Potato Casserole, and the aromatic Bouillabaisse-Inspired Seafood Stew.

Embark on an international journey with Chana Masala Stuffed Bell Peppers, Tandoori Chicken Skewers, and the bold Salt, Pepper & Pasilla Buffalo Wings. Allow the Zen Macrobiotic Bowl to guide you toward mindful dining, and relish the decadence of Chocolate Zucchini Power Clusters and Almond Tiramisu.

May these recipes serve as an ongoing source of joy, inspiration, and connection in your own culinary pursuits. Happy cooking, my fellow gastronomes!

- Andrew West, 2024

Index of Recipes by Page

6. Shellfish and Sea Vegetable Three Sisters Stew
7. Johnnycakes with Rosemary Brown Butter
8. Ash Cake with Berry Compote with Lavender
9. Hoecakes- Refined Version with Cider Reduction Glaze
10. Clam Chowder with Bacon and Leek Clam Chowder Variation
11 Pepper Pot Soup with Hard Cider and Apple Tripe Stew Variation
12 Apple Tansey with Dried Fruit and Citrus Zest Infusion Variation
13 Asparagus and Hazelnut Succotash
14 Pemmican (Native American influence)
15 Hasty Pudding
15b. Vanilla Bean and Berries Hasty Pudding
16. New England Boiled Dinner with Mustard and Brown Sugar Glaze Variation
17. Brunswick Stew
18. Chicken Pot Pie
19. Cornbread
20. Shoo Fly Pie
21. Gumbo
22. Sally Lunn Buns
23. Spoonbread with Classic Caramelized Onion Gravy
24. (Mock) Terrapin Soup
25. Apple Pandowdy
26. Hoppin' John
27. Southern Biscuits and Gravy
28. Shrimp & Grits
29. Jambalaya
30. Fried Green Tomatoes
31. Boiled Peanuts
32. Sonker (North Carolina dessert)
33. Red Beans & Rice
34. Baltimore Peach Cake
35. Pickled Watermelon Rind
36. Chicken & Dumplings
37. (Updated) Hardtack + Savoury Variation
38. Molasses Cookies
39. Bean Soup with Sweet Potato Surprise Variation
40. Molasses Taffy
41. Confederate Hash with Mushroom and Swiss Upgrade Variation
42. Tomato & Peach Corn Dodgers
43. Boiled Salted Meat with Coffee and Cocoa Rub Variation
44. Union Pudding with Spiced Apple Compote Variation
45. Salted Cajun Fish Jerky
46. Tomato Marmalade
47. Mushroom Gravy Grits
48. Braised Pork Belly
49. Chess Pie
50. Quick Pickled Okra
51. English Oxtail Consommé
52. Corn & Tomato Salad
53. Bourbon Balls
54. Graham Crackers
55. Slow-Roasted Pork Shoulder, Collard Greens & Pimento Cheese Sandwich
56. Oysters Rockefeller
57. The Waldorf Salad
58. Chicken à la King
59. Parker House Rolls
60. Gumbo Z'Herbes
61. Lobster Newberg

62. The Bourbon Hot Brown
63. Turkey Tetrazzini with Brandy
64. Boston Creme Pie
65. Chicken & Waffles
66. Sam Wo's Wonton Soup
67. Coca-Cola Salad
68. Elevated Chicken à la Maryland
69. Sloppy Joe and Maple-Bacon Joe Variation
70. Homemade Ketchup
71. Homemade Dried Chipped Beef & Creamed Chipped Beef
72. Cauliflower Chicken Divan
73. Potato Kugel
74. Crabmeat Corn Chowder
75. Green Banana Molasses Bread
76. Green Goddess Salad
77. Hay & Straw with Blue Cheese Alfredo Variation
78. Ambrosia Salad
79. Wonder Bread
80. Baby Ruth Bars
81. Candy Techniques for Baby Ruth Bars
82. Ancient Grain Salmon Pie
83. Olive Sandwiches & Our Black Olive & Fig on Croissant
84. Girl Scout Cookies
85. Clams Casino with Whiskey Maple Clams Casino Variation
86. Individual Rum-Infused Pineapple Upside-Down Cakes
87. Deviled Eggs with Caviar
88. Tomato "Jell-O" Salad
89. Lemon Pound Cake
90. Barley, Beer & Cheese Meatloaf
91. Campfire Cast-Iron Stew: White Kidney Bean and Ham Hock
92. Hobo Bread
93. Depression Green Chili Stew
94. Chicago-Style Hot Dog with The Sonoran Dog Variation
95. Sawmill Gravy on Biscuits
96. Corned Beef
97. Deviled Ham
98. Vinegar Pie
99. Water Pie
100. Tuna and Ham Casserole
101. Campfire Canned Oyster Casserole
102. Chicken and Sausage Étouffée
103. Cabbage Soup with Okra and Black-Eyed Peas
104. Mennonite Delicate White Cake
105. Philly Cheesesteak
106. Grandma's Potato Salad
107. Key Lime Pie
108. Chicken-fried Steak
109. Clam Linguine
110. Diner Fried Bologna Sandwich
111. Cheese & Tomato Mashed Potato Pie
112. TV Dinner: Salisbury Steak with Mashed Potatoes and Buttered Flageolets
113. Cuban Sandwich
114. Pineapple Lime Cheese Salad
115. Ham Banana Rolls with Fiesta Fusion Glaze Variation
116. Rumaki
117. Cheesy Beer Green Bean Casserole
118. Fried Catfish
119. Shredded BBQ Chicken & Tater Tot Casserole
120. Spicy Jalapeño and Pepper Jack Frankfurter Soup
121. 1957 Hawaiian Pizza
122. Vegas Shrimp Cocktail
123. Simple Coq au Vin Blanc with Tarragon Mash
124. Sole Meunière with Lemon-Caper Brown Butter

125. Pacific Northwest Salmon Chowder
126. Oregon Hazelnut-Crusted Chicken
127. Manhattan Clam Chow Mein
128. Harlem Renaissance Spiced Sweet Potato Casserole
129. Bouillabaisse-Inspired Seafood Stew
130. Salade Lyonnaise
131. Chana Masala Stuffed Bell Peppers
132. Tandoori Chicken Skewers
133. Salt, Pepper & Pasilla Buffalo Wings
134. Zen Macrobiotic Bowl
135. Chocolate Zucchini Power Clusters
136. Seasonal Stonefruit Galette
137. Herb-Infused Quiche
138. Almond Tiramisu
139. Slow-Cooked Tomato Sauce with Onion and Butter
140. Chicken Liver Pâté
141. Chocolate Orange Mousse
142. Shrimp Scampi
143. Chili Con Queso & Homemade 'Velveeta' Cheese
144. Cajun Cornbread Pudding
145. Cajun Blackened Fish
146. Savory Chicken Lettuce Cups
147. Japanese Clear Onion Soup
148. Grilled Eggplant Lasagna Rolls
149. Pistachio-Raspberry Linzer Torte
150. Baked Brie
151. Turkey Enchilada with Mole Sauce
152. Basil Pesto Sun-Dried Tomato Spinach Dip
153. Quick Boozy Beef Stroganoff
154. Chili-Lime Shrimp Tacos and Avocado Crema
155. Vegetable Wellington
156. Peach Bourbon Glazed Pork Butt
157. Blue Cheese and Walnut Stuffed Grilled Portobellos
158. Asian Fusion Blackberry Salad with Sesame-Crusted Goat Cheese
159. Lobster Dumpling
160. Smoked Salmon and Cream Cheese Avocado Toast
161. Korean BBQ Tacos
162. Lemon Vermicelli with Roasted Garlic and Asiago
163. Lemon Vermicelli with Quick Pickled Vegetables and Pecorino
164. Caribbean Jerk Shrimp and Mango Salsa Bowl
165. Lemongrass Infused Pad See Ew with Rapini and Shrimp
166. Pumpkin & Sage Cauliflower Crust Pizza
167. Ramen Burger
168. Reverse Seared Steak
169. Sakura Blossom Sushi Rice Pudding
170. Aji Amarillo Massaman Curry Beef
171. Meyer Lemon Pork and Grape Skewer Tapas
172. Slow-Cooked Freekeh and Chicken Casserole
173. Herb-Infused Adobo Chicken Burrito
174. Plum and Almond Brownie Bars with Boozy Twist
175. Chocolate-Coconut Stout Barley Pudding
176. Bourbon Pecan Apple Butter
177. Wine-Soaked Tomato Peach Parfait
178. Gazpacho Granita
179. Blue Cheese and Walnut No-Churn Ice Cream
180. Caribbean Spiced Rum Banana Foster Tart